THE EVERYTHING KIDS' NATURE BOOK

Create Clouds, Make Waves, Defy Gravity and Much More!

Kathiann M. Kowalski

Adams Media Corporation
Holbrook, Massachusetts

WHAT PARENTS AND TEACHERS SAY

"*The Everything Kids' Nature Book* invites kids to dive in and explore the natural world. Kids will love this enriching exploration of the world around us!"
Naomi Singer, Newton, MA
Language Arts and Reading Specialist, Grades K–5

"The Everything Kids' Books are fun, challenging, and educational."
Lynn Favreau, RN, mother, homeschooling parent

This book is dedicated to my husband, Michael Meissner.

Published by Adams Media Corporation
260 Center Street, Holbrook, MA 02343 U.S.A.

ISBN: 1-58062-321-2

Printed in the United States of America.

J I H G F E D C B

Library of Congress Cataloging-in-Publication Data
Kowalski, Kathiann M.
The everything kids nature book : create clouds, make waves, defy gravity, and much more! / Kathiann M. Kowalski.
p. cm. -- (An Everything series book)
Includes bibliographical references (p.).
Summary: Explores the different natural habitats--forests, rain forests, grasslands, deserts, cold regions, oceans and rivers--and the plant and animal life that exists in each. Includes related activities and word lists.
ISBN 1-58062-321-2
1. Nature study--Activity programs--Juvenile literature. [1. Nature study.] I. Title. II. Everything series.
QH54.5 .K68 2000
508--dc21 00-026930

NOTE: All activities in this book should be performed with adult supervision. Likewise, common sense and care are essential to the conduct of any and all activities, whether described in this book or otherwise. Parents or guardians should supervise children during outings in any kind of natural habitat.

Cover illustrations by Joseph Sherman.
Interior illustrations by Kathie Kelleher.
Illustrations on pages viii, 16, and 56 by Barry Littmann.

CONTENTS

CONTENTS

INTRODUCTION

Discovering nature is a life-long adventure. Venture into the natural world, and you'll find a wealth of year-round fascination.

Think of this book as a tour guide to start your nature adventure. Its purpose is to help you have fun. Approach nature with curiosity and playfulness. Open yourself to new ideas and experiences. You'll be surprised at how much fun nature offers.

Throughout the book, you'll find dozens of "Get Active!" projects. Enjoy these activities, and you'll discover more about nature firsthand. Adult supervision is recommended, and remember to always use common sense precautions. For safety's sake, always bring an adult along when you go on any kind of nature outing.

Chapter 1 introduces you to our world and its natural phenomena. Learn about planet Earth, natural disasters, sunrise, sunset, and the seasons. Earth is just right for life!

Chapter 2 addresses the diversity of life. First come single-celled organisms. Then come all sorts of fungi and plants. Animals include organisms without a backbone, plus fishes, amphibians, reptiles, birds, and mammals.

Chapters 3 through 8 introduce you to different kinds of habitats. Habitats are the environments where living things make their homes. Learn about the natural habitats near your home. Also learn about the habitats in other parts of your country and the world.

The United States, for example, has practically every major habitat. There are warm rain forests in Hawaii and frozen tundra plains in northern Alaska. There are vast areas of other forests, grasslands, and deserts too. Canada also has a great variety of natural habitats.

Both countries also have thousands of miles of coastlines, plus thousands of lakes, rivers, and streams. These provide a variety of marine environments.

Chapter 9 shows you how people affect nature. Our world's valuable resources are limited. Plus, many species are threatened or endangered. Learn how you can help protect the environment.

Chapter 10 encourages you to enjoy the great outdoors. Hiking and camping are great ways to experience nature. Also enjoy art, writing, gardening, and other activities outdoors. As you enjoy the natural world, respect the environment and its creatures.

Speaking of creatures, check out the "Featured Creature" boxes throughout this book. They're packed with information about bats, beavers, mudpuppies, rattlesnakes, toucans, pandas, and over a dozen other animals.

Other boxes include "It's a Natural Fact!" and "Nature Stats." Share this information with family and friends. They'll be astounded by your knowledge.

"Words to Know" are highlighted throughout the book. They're also explained in the glossary near the end.

After you read this book, take your nature adventures further. Try out the activities suggested in each chapter. Also check out the resources and organizations listed at the end of the book. Pursue a love of nature, and you'll constantly discover new realms of wonder.

So, read through and enjoy *The Everything Kids' Nature Book*. Enjoy discovering everything you can about nature!

CHAPTER 1
THE WORLD OF NATURE

WHERE IS NATURE?

Thundering hoofs carry a herd of horned wildebeests across Africa's Serengeti Plain. During the rainy season, grasses provide abundant food. But in the dry season, the herd must look elsewhere for water and food. Thus, the herd migrates across the vast plain. Migration is a seasonal travel pattern.

Most of the time the wildebeests walk with a rocking-horse gait. Yet looming danger may make the group charge. If a lurking lion separates one unfortunate wildebeest from the herd, the kill means a meal for the lion.

Halfway around the world from the Serengeti, toucans call to each other in Costa Rica's rain forest. Monkeys swing from tree to tree. On the ground, a giant anteater breaks open an ant mound with its powerful front claws. Then the anteater extends its sticky, two-foot tongue. Moments later, it eats a tasty insect snack.

All sorts of foliage, fruits, and flowers grow in the rain forest. The plants, in turn, provide homes for thousands of animals. There are brilliant blue butterflies, trotting pachyberas, and slow-moving sloths.

Thousands of miles away, the Arctic summer brings bursts of bright purple saxifrage flowers to the tundra. Yellow cinquefoils, white heather, and creamy mountain avens flowers also dot the landscape in Canada's Nunavut Territory. Temperatures get bitterly cold here. Even in July and August, temperatures may dip below freezing.

migration: seasonal travel pattern for animals. [mye-GRAY-shun]

oblate ellipsoid: geometrical term to describe Earth's squashed sphere shape. [OHB-late ee-LIP-soyd]

vacuum: empty space. [VACK-yoo-um]

IT'S A NATURAL FACT!

What Shape Is Our World In?

The Earth is round, right? Or is it?

Earth is a sphere, but it's slightly flattened at the poles. It also bulges at the equator. The technical term for the shape is an **oblate ellipsoid**. For all practical purposes, let's just say the Earth is round.

Yet life survives. Mosses, lichens, and about two hundred species of flowering plants thrive despite the cold. Caribou, musk oxen, wolves, foxes, and other animals roam this Arctic land.

A few months later, in the northeastern United States, cool, crisp air and brilliantly colored leaves signal fall's arrival. Soon the leaves will turn brown and fall to the ground. Squirrels busily gather nuts. Bears and raccoons find sheltered places to rest during winter.

Each of these scenes gives a different view of nature. Nature is our world and the many things that live there. It is exotic life in faraway places. Nature is also as close as your back yard or the neighborhood park.

Nature is even in the crowded city. Trees line city streets or grow in parks. Pigeons and other birds flutter about. Even pesky insects and other critters are part of nature in the city. (We just want them to stay out of our homes!)

Our world is vast, and so is the world of nature.

OUR WORLD: JUST RIGHT FOR LIFE

Remember the story of Goldilocks and the three bears? Goldilocks tried each bowl of porridge. One was too hot. One was too cold. Finally, she found the one that was just right.

Luckily for us, conditions for life on Earth are just right. Earth is the third planet in our solar system. It is 93 million miles (149 million km) from the sun. If it were closer, Earth would be too hot for life to survive. If it were much farther away, it would be way too cold.

Water also makes Earth just right for life. Liquid water lets molecules easily come into contact. This helps chemical reactions needed for life.

Water also makes up an important part of living things. About 90 percent of your own body is water.

Earth also has the right atmosphere for life. As nature writer Rachel Carson put it, we live in an "ocean of air." It ranges from the Earth's surface upwards toward space.

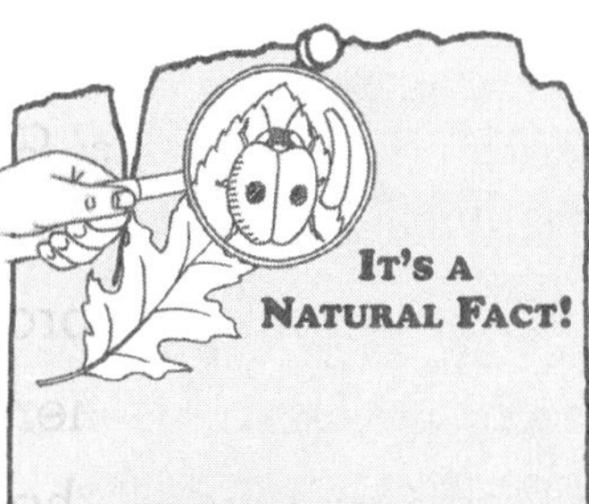

It's a Natural Fact!

No Vacuums Here!

You've probably heard the saying, "Nature abhors a **vacuum**." It doesn't mean you shouldn't clean your room. Rather, it means that life grows almost anywhere.

Even in a built-up neighborhood, you'll likely see grass sprouting through sidewalk cracks. And if your family has a garden, you know how quickly weeds sprout there! Weeds are plants that grow where people don't want them. But even weeds are part of nature.

By volume, air is about 77 percent nitrogen and 21 percent oxygen. We and many other animals need oxygen to breathe. Other chemicals in the air are argon, carbon dioxide, hydrogen, neon, helium, krypton, and xenon. Water vapor—evaporated water—is also in the air.

The atmosphere acts like a blanket. It captures just enough of the sun's warmth and holds it in. Without the atmosphere, Earth's sunny side would be way too hot, and its dark side would be bitterly cold.

The atmosphere is also a sunscreen. Its ozone layer screens out many of the sun's harmful ultraviolet rays.

Our distance from the sun and the presence of water and atmosphere are all just right on Earth. They help life thrive on our planet.

MAKING MOUNTAINS

Scientists believe Earth was formed 4.5 billion years ago. Earth's inner core is solid rock. Surrounding it is an outer core of molten, or melted, rock.

Around the core is the mantle layer. Above the mantle lies Earth's crust. Beneath some parts of the ocean, the crust is only about five miles deep. Under some mountain ranges, however, it's 50 miles (80 km) deep.

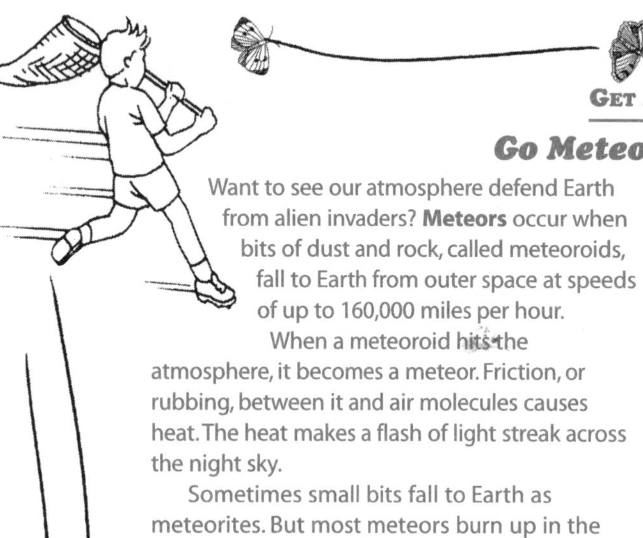

GET ACTIVE!

Go Meteor Watching

Want to see our atmosphere defend Earth from alien invaders? **Meteors** occur when bits of dust and rock, called meteoroids, fall to Earth from outer space at speeds of up to 160,000 miles per hour.

When a meteoroid hits the atmosphere, it becomes a meteor. Friction, or rubbing, between it and air molecules causes heat. The heat makes a flash of light streak across the night sky.

Sometimes small bits fall to Earth as meteorites. But most meteors burn up in the atmosphere. You'll see the most meteor activity during a meteor shower. Dates for three of the most active showers seen north of the equator are:

SHOWER	DATES	PEAK
Quadrantids	January 1-6	January 4
Perseids	July 25-August 18	August 12
Geminids	December 7-15	December 14

Other showers occur too. Watch the news, or check with a local museum or astronomy group.

The best time and place to watch is after midnight in a dark, open area. Bring an adult along for safety. And bundle up warmly, especially during fall or winter.

The crust is divided into fifteen areas, called **tectonic plates**. Rising above the oceans on the plates are the seven continents: Asia, Africa, North America, South America, Europe, Australia, and Antarctica.

The plates "float" on top of the mantle. Sometimes when Earth's plates collided, they pushed the ground up, forming majestic mountains.

The Himalayas in Nepal, India, and China are Earth's tallest mountains. They began forming over 30 million years ago. Mount Everest is the highest peak at 29,030 feet (8,850 m)—over five miles high!

The Rocky Mountains, Alps, Appalachians, Andes, and Ural Mountains also formed from plate movement. When you see a mountain scene, think about how long it took to create each magnificent peak.

WORDS to KNOW

meteor: flash of light that occurs when dust and rock from space, called meteoroids, burns up in Earth's atmosphere. [MEET-ee-or]

tectonic plates: large masses of Earth that "float" on top of the mantle. [tec-TONN-ik PLATES]

volcano: land or underwater formation where pressure has pushed molten rock through the Earth's crust. [vol-KAY-noh]

tsunami: giant wave, usually caused by an earthquake or volcanic eruption. [SOO-nam-ee]

NATURAL DISASTER: VOLCANOES

Volcanoes look like mountains. But instead of being pushed up gradually, volcanoes form when part of Earth's inside gets out. Earth's core is very hot—about 4,500 degrees Celsius (°C). Heat causes molten rock to rise. The molten rock needs somewhere to go.

Volcanoes erupt when mounting pressure breaks through the Earth's crust. In the most violent eruptions, huge black clouds of lava, ash, and dust spit out from the top. Molten lava races along the ground, burning everything in its path. Volcanic eruptions can also trigger earthquakes and giant waves, called **tsunamis**.

Volcanoes build up land surface, but eruptions can also be deadly. Mount Soufriere's eruptions during the 1990s destroyed most homes on the Caribbean island of Montserrat. A 1985 volcanic eruption killed 23,000 people in Colombia. The Krakatoa eruption in Indonesia in 1883 killed over 36,000 people.

NATURAL DISASTER: EARTHQUAKES

Just as the World Series game was to start on October 17, 1989, people at San Francisco's Candlestick Park felt a rumbling. It was an earthquake along California's San Andreas fault. The earthquake killed 67 people in the San Francisco Bay area.

Earthquakes occur most often near edges of tectonic plates. The edges are called **fault lines**. Plates slipping or scraping against each other release energy inside the Earth.

Earthquakes may last only a minute, but they can do tremendous damage. Thousands of people died in 1999 after major earthquakes struck Turkey, Greece, and Taiwan.

Scientists measure earthquakes with two scales. The Richter scale gauges how much energy was released at the earthquake's source. Each whole number on the Richter scale is a tenfold increase over the previous number. Level 2 is barely detectable. Level 6 is moderately destructive. Level 8 is total damage.

The modified Mercalli scale ranges from I through XII. It describes how an earthquake is felt at a specific place. Level I earthquakes are barely felt. Level VI earthquakes are felt by everyone.

If everything around you starts shaking and rumbling, duck and cover. Duck down under a desk or in a doorway. Cover your head with your arms. When the rumbling stops, get outside. Wait until an adult says the building is safe before going back inside.

WORDS to KNOW

earthquake: release of energy inside Earth, generally caused by tectonic plates scraping or sliding against each other.

fault lines: borders between tectonic plates.

mass: how much matter something has.

kilogram: metric measure of weight, equal to 1,000 grams. [KILL-oh-gram]

ultraviolet: light wavelengths shorter than the visible spectrum. [ULL-tra-VYE-let]

NATURE STATS

How Does Earth Measure Up?

The distance around the equator is 24,902 miles (40,075 km). Measuring around the poles, the distance is 24,860 miles (40,008 km). The distance from the North Pole to the South Pole through the center of the Earth is 7,900 miles (12,714 km).

Mass measures how much matter something has. Scientists have calculated Earth's mass at 6.0×10^{24} **kilograms**. That would be 6 followed by 24 zeroes, or six trillion trillion. No wonder the ancient Roman character Atlas looks so tired in pictures that show him carrying the world on his shoulders!

It's a Natural Fact!

Hawaii: Built by Volcanoes

The Hawaiian Islands were built by volcanic action on the floor of the Pacific Ocean. Some of the islands' volcanoes are still active.

In fact, the island chain continues to change. Islands to the southeast are younger, geologically speaking. They are still growing.

NATURAL PHENOMENA: SUNRISE AND SUNSET

At sunrise, a glowing red ball peeks above the eastern horizon. As it rises, it shades to orange and then yellow. The day dawns bright and full of hope.

Just as awesome is the sparkling palette that sunset paints across the sky. While the eastern sky may still be deep blue, streaks of orange, pink, and red light the western sky. Like a glowing ball, the sun sinks lower and lower. Finally, it slips below the horizon.

NEVER look directly at the sun. No matter what time of the day it is, harmful **ultraviolet** rays can damage your eyes. Instead, focus away from the sun on the rest of the sky.

Get Active!

Tectonic Pasta

You need:
2 uncooked lasagna noodles
wide pot with water

NOTE: Use caution with all kitchen appliances. Get adult supervision while using the stove.

1. Break the noodles into 12 pieces. Imagine that your noodles are continents sitting on tectonic plates, and that the water is Earth's mantle of molten rock.
2. Float the pieces on top of the water. Bump them against each other to demonstrate mountain building. Make them move away from each other to show continental spread. Rub them against each other to mimic an earthquake.
3. Put the noodles on a plate. Boil the water. Then carefully put the noodles back in the pot. Lower the heat slightly so the water won't boil over.
4. Pressure from heat currents makes the water bubble up. Inside the earth, pressure from heat currents makes volcanoes erupt. Heat currents make the boiling water move the noodles around.
5. After about 14 minutes, turn off the heat. Remove the noodles with a slotted spoon. Add butter and parsley. Then enjoy your tectonic pasta.

It's a Natural Fact!

The Green Flash

Does the sky ever look green? Yes, but very rarely.

The green flash sometimes happens literally "in a flash." Just before sunrise or just after sunset light's reddish rays may be hidden below the horizon, while the blue hues get scattered by the air. That leaves the green rays, whose wavelengths lie between red and blue. We usually don't see the green flash. Dust and pollution can hide the flash. Trees, buildings, and anything else on the horizon can also hide it.

What causes sunrise and sunset? Although the sun seems to move, it's really Earth that's moving. Earth always spins, or rotates, toward the east.

Unless clouds block the sun, the sky usually looks blue. In fact, however, sunlight contains all colors of light. Red, orange, yellow, green, blue, indigo, and violet make up the visible spectrum of light. Put them all together, and you get white.

Different colors of light have different wavelengths. A wavelength is the distance between one wave crest, or top, and the next one. Violet, indigo, and blue have the shortest wavelengths. Red, orange, and yellow have longer wavelengths.

You and a friend can demonstrate wavelengths by holding two ends of a rope. Move one end slowly from side to side for long wavelengths. Wiggle it quickly for shorter wavelengths.

As light waves enter the atmosphere, they strike gas and particle molecules in the air. The molecules scatter the light. That is, they split the different colors apart. This phenomenon is called **Rayleigh scattering**.

The shorter bluish wavelengths get scattered about four times more easily than the longer reddish wavelengths. Because they reach our eyes from all directions in the sky, the sky looks blue.

Near sunrise and sunset, however, the sun's rays must travel through more of the atmosphere to reach us. By then, most bluish wavelengths are scattered away. The longer red wavelengths make the sky glow orange or red.

WHAT MAKES THE COLORS IN A RAINBOW?

If you have a prism, you can separate sunlight into its individual colors. A typical prism looks like a triangular column of glass. As light passes through, the glass bends the

Rayleigh scattering: process by which molecules in the atmosphere split or scatter different colors within white light. [RALL-ee SKAT-er-ing]

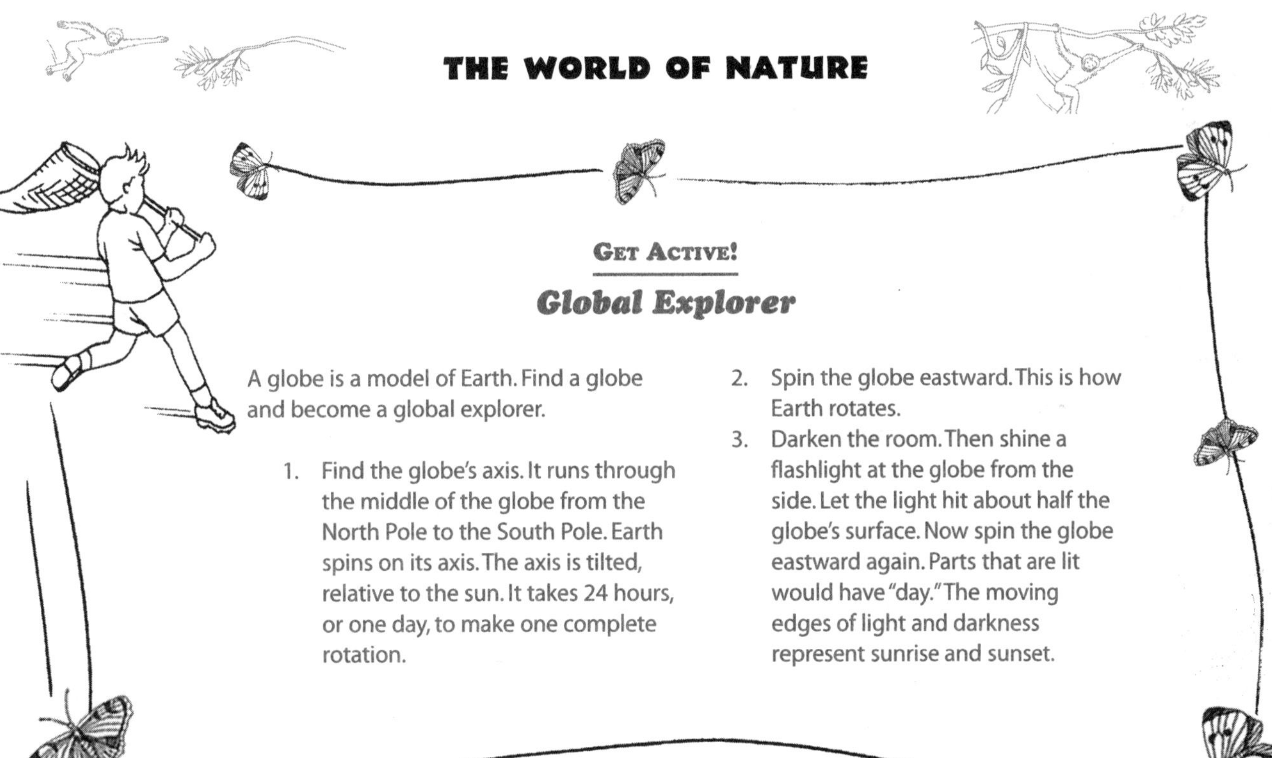

GET ACTIVE!

Global Explorer

A globe is a model of Earth. Find a globe and become a global explorer.

1. Find the globe's axis. It runs through the middle of the globe from the North Pole to the South Pole. Earth spins on its axis. The axis is tilted, relative to the sun. It takes 24 hours, or one day, to make one complete rotation.
2. Spin the globe eastward. This is how Earth rotates.
3. Darken the room. Then shine a flashlight at the globe from the side. Let the light hit about half the globe's surface. Now spin the globe eastward again. Parts that are lit would have "day." The moving edges of light and darkness represent sunrise and sunset.

light. The bending lets you see the visible spectrum: red, orange, yellow, green, blue, indigo, and violet.

Rainbows result from nature's prisms. Sometimes after it stops raining overhead, droplets stay in the air ahead of you. If sun shines from behind you through the droplets, the drops act like prisms.

But light's reddish wavelengths are longer than the bluish wavelengths. They arch over the shorter wavelengths. This makes the rainbow curve.

Don't search for a pot of gold at the end of the rainbow! As you move, the projection of the rainbow moves too. When the air dries, the rainbow disappears.

CHANGING SEASONS

Do you have a favorite season? Spring's budding leaves, bright flowers, and warmer days bring new life. It's a great time to play outdoors, plant a garden, or watch a baseball game.

Hot summer days are great for swimming or playing at the beach. Sometimes a thunderstorm brings welcome relief from the heat.

Autumn days are crisp and cool. Tree leaves change to yellow, orange, red, and brown. Days get shorter.

The sun sets early in winter. Sledding, skating, and building snowmen are great fun on a cold winter day.

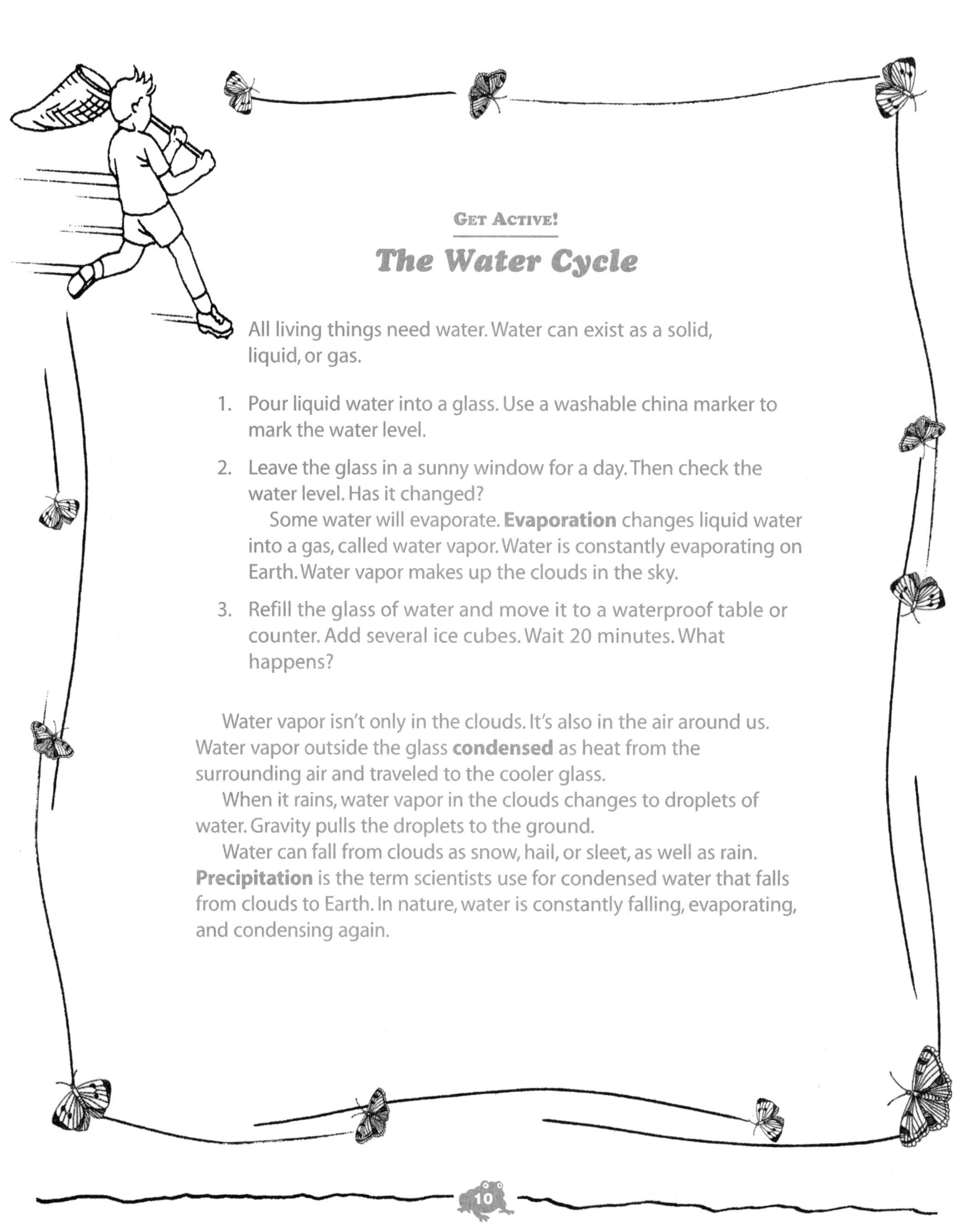

GET ACTIVE!

The Water Cycle

All living things need water. Water can exist as a solid, liquid, or gas.

1. Pour liquid water into a glass. Use a washable china marker to mark the water level.
2. Leave the glass in a sunny window for a day. Then check the water level. Has it changed?

   Some water will evaporate. **Evaporation** changes liquid water into a gas, called water vapor. Water is constantly evaporating on Earth. Water vapor makes up the clouds in the sky.
3. Refill the glass of water and move it to a waterproof table or counter. Add several ice cubes. Wait 20 minutes. What happens?

Water vapor isn't only in the clouds. It's also in the air around us. Water vapor outside the glass **condensed** as heat from the surrounding air and traveled to the cooler glass.

When it rains, water vapor in the clouds changes to droplets of water. Gravity pulls the droplets to the ground.

Water can fall from clouds as snow, hail, or sleet, as well as rain. **Precipitation** is the term scientists use for condensed water that falls from clouds to Earth. In nature, water is constantly falling, evaporating, and condensing again.

But wait! Not everyone experiences the seasons this way. While brisk December winds sweep across North Dakota, Los Angeles often gets warm, sunny days with temperatures over 75 degrees Fahrenheit (°F). As New Englanders swelter from summer heat, Alaska can still have temperatures close to freezing.

Strangely enough, Earth is nearest the sun around January 3. Yet at that time, areas in the Northern Hemisphere have winter. Why?

If you shine a flashlight directly at a wall, you'll see a bright spot. Angle it, and you'll cover a broader area with a dimmer beam.

The same thing happens with Earth. As Earth orbits the sun, its axis stays tilted. During summer, the sun's rays strike the Northern Hemisphere directly. It receives more light and heat.

Also during summer, the tilt brings more areas within the sun's range. Thus, summer days are longer and brighter.

In winter, the Northern Hemisphere tilts away from the sun. Light falls indirectly, at an angle. Temperatures fall as days get shorter.

What happens in the Southern Hemisphere? Because of Earth's tilt, seasons there are reversed. December brings the start of summer to Australia. Winter starts in June.

Even in summer, it's cooler in Alaska than it is in Florida. Distance from the equator makes the difference. Polar regions always get the sun's rays at a slant, so they stay cold year round!

WORDS to KNOW

evaporation: process by which liquid water changes into water vapor. [ee-vap-or-AY-shun]

condensation: process by which water changes from a gas into a liquid. [con-den-SAY-shun]

precipitation: collective term for rain, snow, sleet, hail, or other forms of water falling to Earth. [pree-SIP-ih-TAY-shun]

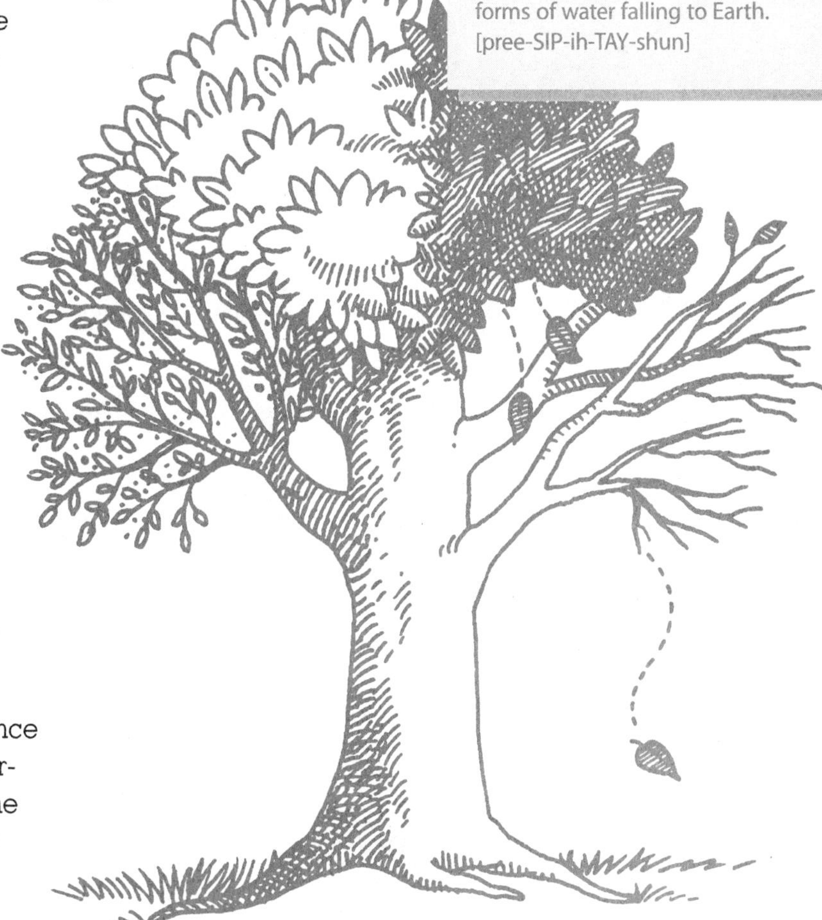

WORDS to KNOW

altitude: height above sea level. [AL-tih-tood]

habitat: environment in which a living thing makes its home. [HAB-ih-tat]

In contrast, direct sunlight brings more light and heat to areas near the equator. That means warmer weather all year round.

Prevailing winds, **altitude** (land height above sea level), nearness to lakes or oceans, and other factors also affect an area's weather. One tropical area may be a rain forest, while another is a desert.

Habitats are areas where living things make their homes. Temperature, rainfall, and other factors produce a variety of habitats. Each habitat plays an important part in the world of nature.

CHAPTER 2
THE NATURE OF LIFE

HOW DO YOU KNOW IF SOMETHING IS ALIVE?

You're alive. A goldfish is alive, and so is a tree. In contrast, a rock is not alive. Nor is a tank of oxygen gas or a bottle of pure water.

Sometimes the answer isn't so obvious. An underwater coral reef looks like beautiful rock, but its growing parts house living coral polyps. A fire's flame jumps and dances, but it is not alive.

All living things are made of cells. **DNA**, or deoxyribonucleic acid, is a chemical found in cells. The precise makeup of something's DNA decides whether it will be a mushroom, cabbage, frog, lion, or some other form of life.

Living things have a **metabolism**. They get chemicals from some sort of food to their cells and turn them into energy. To do this, humans and other animals need oxygen. They get the oxygen through a process called **respiration**.

Living things **eliminate** waste. Mammals do this by exhaling, sweating, and going to the bathroom.

Living things grow. Living things also **reproduce**. They produce other organisms of the same kind.

Living things also respond to their environment. If you are cold, you put on a sweater. Move a plant away from the window, and it will grow toward the light.

All living things do these processes. Yet, there is still lots of variety among the living things on Earth.

WORDS to KNOW

DNA: deoxyribonucleic acid, which is the chemical in each cell that contains its genetic information.

metabolism: process by which a living thing gets some sort of food into its cells and turns it into energy. [meh-TAB-oh-lism]

respiration: extracting oxygen from the air and getting it to cells; breathing. [res-pihr-AY-shun]

eliminate: get rid of. [ee-LIM-in-ate]

reproduce: process by which a living thing duplicates itself and/or its cells. [ree-proh-DOOS]

CLASSIFYING NATURAL LIFE

What's that in your back yard? Someone from France would call it *un arbre*. A Mexican person would call it *el árbol*. You would call it a tree.

But what kind of tree is it? Is it an oak tree, a sugar maple, an elm, an aspen, or a dogwood?

Scientists who study life are called **biologists**. They like living things to have precise names. That way, other biologists know just what they are talking about.

The special naming system biologists use is called **taxonomy**. Taxonomy classifies life forms at seven different levels: kingdom, phylum, class, order, family, genus, and species.

Kingdom is the broadest group. It places a life form into its broadest category. Each other level gets more and more specific. The most specific level is **species**. In nature, members of a species reproduce only with members of the same species.

WORDS to KNOW

biologist: scientist who studies living things. [bye-OL-oh-jist]

taxonomy: scientific classification of living things. [TAX-on-oh-mee]

species: a specific type of living thing; the most specific level of description in taxonomy. The term generally describes organisms that reproduce only by themselves or with each other in nature to produce fertile offspring. [SPEE-shees]

GET ACTIVE!

Life in a Drop of Water

Is there a pond near your home? Find an area near the edge where the water seems still. Collect a cup of the water in a clear, recycled soda bottle.

Examine a drop of the water under a microscope. You'll probably see some tiny things moving. Thousands of microscopic organisms can live in a cup of pond water. Microscopic life lives in every habitat around the world.

Featured Creature

Panda Puzzle

Giant pandas puzzled scientists for a long time. Were these huge, furry, and tubby creatures bears? Or were the masked white and black animals more like raccoons?

Giant pandas do look like bears. They climb trees like bears. Their blood and some inner organs are like those of bears. But giant pandas' skulls are heavier than typical bear skulls. Their muzzles are shorter. Their teeth, jaws, feet, and legs are different.

Giant pandas' wristbones were strange too. Giant pandas use the bone like a sixth finger or thumb. It helps them grab things. Only the red panda, or lesser panda, has a wristbone similar to the giant panda. With its red coat, white face, and bushy tail, the red panda certainly looks like a raccoon.

Finally in the 1980s, scientists made a decision. After studying the giant pandas' genes up close, they decided it was more closely related to bears. Because of the differences, it has its own "subfamily" classification and the scientific name, *Ailuropoda malanoleuca.*

Scientists decided that the red panda was more closely related to raccoons. It has its own subfamily classification too. Its scientific name is *Ailurus fulgens.*

Now that scientists know what they are, giant pandas face another challenge. As people moved into the lower ranges of China's mountains during the twentieth century, they cut down many bamboo trees. Bamboo is the giant panda's favorite food. As their food supply dwindled, the number of giant pandas in the wild dipped below 1,000. The species became endangered. Now the World Wildlife Fund, the Chinese government, and other groups are working to help the giant panda survive.

The scientific name of an **organism** is the Latin form of its genus and species. You, for example, are a member of the species, *Homo sapiens*. A grasshopper is *Schistocerca americana*.

THE SIMPLE LIFE: MONERA AND PROTISTA

Monera and *Protista* are kingdoms of single-celled organisms. Living in ponds, oceans, soil, and practically everywhere on Earth, they play a crucial role in nature.

Some simple life forms have **chlorophyll**. They can make their own food. This process, which is also used by all green plants, is called **photosynthesis**. The organism uses sunlight and carbon dioxide to make a simple sugar plus oxygen.

Life forms that can't do this generally feed on other organisms. This way, they indirectly benefit from the sun's energy.

Most life survives in a fairly narrow range of living conditions. Temperatures generally must be above freezing and below 170°F (77°C). The surrounding environment can't be too salty, nor do most life forms tolerate strong acids or bases. These are chemicals like chlorine bleach and vinegar (acids) or ammonia (base).

But life turns up in all sorts of places. Bacteria have adapted to the frigid cold of the polar regions.

At the other extreme, scientists have found single-celled organisms in Yellowstone National Park's hot springs and also near lava flows from volcanoes. Microscopic organisms have even been found in rocks and caves far below the ground.

Some simple life forms provide food and nutrients for other organisms. Others help break down other material. Bacteria are used this way at sewage treatment plants.

WORDS to KNOW

organism: a living thing. [OR-gun-ism]

chlorophyll: green material in plants and certain bacteria that enables them to make their own food. [KLOR-oh-fill]

photosynthesis: process by which an organism with chlorophyll makes food in the presence of sunlight and water. [FOH-toh-SIN-the-siss]

Simple life forms may even help other organisms stay healthy. Normal bacteria and other organisms inside your intestines keep you well. Even the tiniest life forms do important work in nature.

THE FUNGUS AMONG US

Do you enjoy mushrooms in your salad or on a burger? Mushrooms are a type of life called **fungus**. Over 65,000 kinds of fungi exist in nature.

Are you having a sandwich made with bread for lunch? Bread owes its light, airy texture to yeast. Yeast is another type of fungus.

Not all fungus is so friendly and appealing. Leave a loaf of bread in the cupboard too long, and bluish mold starts to grow. Miss cleaning your bathroom, and mold and mildew mount. Whether it's black, red, or fluffy white, the stuff can get pretty gross!

Where do the fungi come from? Most fungi start from spores—tiny reproductive cells. Spores are often blown around by the air. If they land where conditions are right, they start to grow.

Fungi can be as small as a single cell. Yeast is one example.

Fungi can also be huge. One organism found in northern Michigan, *Armillaria bulbosa*, spread through 15,000 square meters of forest soil. One meter is about 39 inches. Scientists figured that the 1,500-year-old fungus weighed more than 10,000 kilograms, or 11 tons.

WORDS to KNOW

fungus: member of a kingdom of living things that can be single or multi-celled, but which do not make their own food. [FUNG-us]

digestion: process of breaking food down into useful nutrients. [dye-JES-chun]

parasite: an organism that feeds off another without giving its host any benefit. [PAIR-uh-site]

symbiotic: mutually beneficial. [sim-bye-OT-ik]

Many fungi feed on dead things. Fungi play a crucial role in nature. They decompose dead trees, leaves, and other plant and animal material. This way, the nutrients can be used again for new life.

But fungus **digestion** is weird. Fungi digest food outside their bodies. They give off chemicals that break down the food. Then the fungus' individual cells absorb the nutrients.

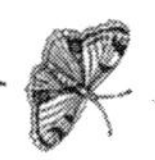

GET ACTIVE!

Get Vascular

Unlike you, plants don't have hearts to pump fluids through their bodies. So how does a plant's vascular tubing get water from the roots to the leaves? The answer is capillary action—the attraction by which a solid, such as a tube, sucks up a liquid. See for yourself how it works.

You need:
clear glass
water
food dye
fresh stalk of celery

1. Fill the glass half full of water. Add a few drops of food dye.
2. Carefully trim top and bottom ends of celery stalk. It should be taller than the glass.
3. Put the celery in the colored water. Place the glass where no one will disturb it for several hours.
4. After several hours, look at the celery. The top should show some of the dye's coloring. Capillary action pulled the colored water from the glass up through the celery's vascular tubing.

Some fungi are **parasites**. They feed off living things, without providing any benefits. Athlete's foot is one example.

Still other fungi feed on living things, but they provide a benefit to the host. Scientists call this a **symbiotic** relationship.

Lichens are one example of a symbiotic relationship. Lichens are really two organisms that grow together—a fungus and a type of algae. The fungus gives the algae a place to live. The algae uses photosynthesis to make food for itself and the fungus.

Other fungi have symbiotic relationships with trees. Growing on roots, the fungi get food from the trees. In return, the fungi provide nutrients that help the trees fight frost and drought.

PLANTS: PUTTING DOWN ROOTS

Scientists say at least 300,000 different types of plants exist today. Plants provide us with food, shelter, and even clothing.

Nearly all plants live on land. They hold themselves in place with roots. Roots also absorb water from the soil.

Almost all plants make their own food through photosynthesis. Parts of the plant contain a green substance called

chlorophyll. These parts combine carbon dioxide and water in the presence of sunlight to make sugar and release oxygen.

Not all plants make seeds. Walk through a forest, and you'll see moss growing on trees or rocks. The 10,000 species of moss are a type of plant called bryophyte. They reproduce by making spores, similar to fungi.

Seedless **vascular** plants also make spores. Vascular means the plant has "tubing." The tubing gets water from the roots to the leaves where the plant makes food. The 12,000 species of ferns are seedless vascular plants.

Other plants reproduce from seeds. Many, but not all, seed-bearing plants make their seeds in flowers.

vascular: relating to tubes that transport liquid within an organism. [VAS-kyeh-lehr]

invertebrate: animal with no backbone. [in-VER-teh-brate]

vertebrate: animal with a backbone. [VER-teh-brate]

ANIMALS OF ALL SORTS

The animal kingdom is vast. It includes the tiniest beetle and the giant blue whale in the ocean. It includes sponges, worms, insects, fish, lizards, frogs, birds, tigers, and even you!

Backbones make a big difference to biologists who classify life forms. **Invertebrates** have no backbone. **Vertebrates** do.

Some invertebrates are soft and squishy. Earthworms and jellyfish are two examples. Other invertebrates have an outer covering. Shrimp, snails, and clams have shells, for example. Insects have a hard substance, called *chitin*, covering their bodies. The chitin holds their inner organs together and protects them.

Fish are animals with backbones. Some, like sharks, live in seawater. Others, like trout, have freshwater homes. Fish absorb oxygen from the water through their gills. They reproduce by laying eggs.

Amphibians are vertebrates. They change form as they mature.

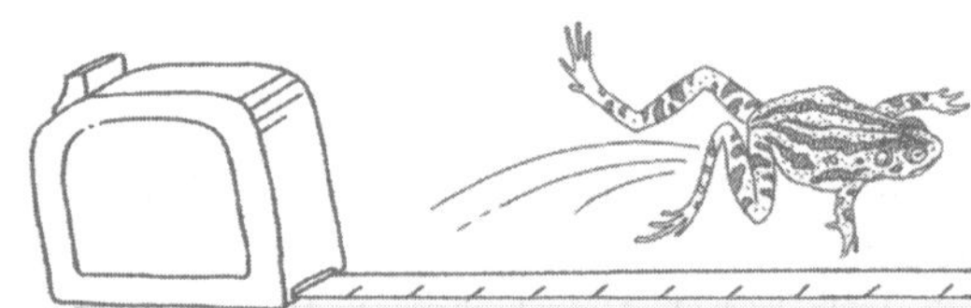

NATURE STATS

Many, Many Species

Scientists have identified over 9,000 species of birds, 4,000 species of mammals, 6,000 reptiles, 4,000 amphibians, and 45,000 fishes. And these are just the animals with backbones! Nature's diversity is truly amazing!

A frog, for example, begins its life by swimming around as a tadpole. As it matures, it begins to grow legs. When it's ready, the adult frog hops out of the pond to live on land. When it's time to reproduce, frogs lay eggs in water. The eggs will hatch into new tadpoles.

Reptiles are also vertebrates. They hatch from eggs and breathe air into their lungs. Scales cover their bodies. Snakes, alligators, and lizards are examples of reptiles.

Birds are animals of a different feather altogether. Most birds fly by flapping their wings, although some, like penguins and ostriches, do not fly. Birds' beaks, feet, and bodies seem to come in all shapes and sizes. Young birds hatch from eggs.

Mammals are another class of vertebrates. Mammals have hair on their bodies instead of scales or feathers. Also, unlike other animals, almost all mammals are born alive, not hatched from eggs. Animal mothers nurse their babies with milk from their mammary glands.

Dogs, tigers, chimps, horses, and rabbits are examples of mammals. You are a mammal too.

Fish, amphibians, and reptiles are all cold-blooded. This means that their bodies are the same temperature as the area around them.

Birds and mammals, on the other hand, are warm-blooded. Their bodies control their own temperature. Your normal temperature is 98.6°F.

metamorphosis: significant change in body form as an organism changes from an immature animal into an adult [met-uh-MOR-foh-siss]

CHAINS, WEBS, AND PYRAMIDS

Only certain single-celled organisms and green plants make their own food. Photosynthesis uses sunlight, water, and carbon dioxide to make simple sugar. Oxygen is given off as a byproduct. Living things that make their own food are called primary producers.

It's a Natural Fact!

Amphibians and Change

"Amphibian" comes from the Greek words *amphis*, meaning double or two-sided, and *bios*, meaning life. "Amphibians are organisms with double or two lives," explains Alan Richmond at the University of Massachusetts in Amherst.

The first part of the amphibian's life is the larval stage. Then it undergoes **metamorphosis**, or change, to achieve its adult form.

Often the change is complete, as with frogs and toads. Most amphibians develop lungs to breathe air, plus legs to move around on land. Scientists speculate that amphibians were the first animals with backbones to live on land.

Other times, the amphibian keeps certain traits from its larval stage, like gills or certain skin features. Then the metamorphosis is said to be partial.

WORDS to KNOW

food chain: term used to describe who-eats-whom relationships in nature.

food web: term used to describe multiple relationships among predators and prey in nature.

carnivore: meat-eating animal. [KAR-nih-vor]

herbivore: plant-eating animal. [ER-bih-vor]

food pyramid: method for depicting how certain organisms in a habitat support other organisms higher up on the pyramid.

nocturnal: active at night. [nock-TER-nul]

ecological niche: an organism's "place" in its habitat, such as the time of day it's active or its specific feeding pattern. [EEK-oh-loj-ik-ul NISH]

echolocation: method bats use to locate prey with sound waves. [EK-oh-loh-CAY-shun]

Any living thing that can't make its own food must get it from elsewhere. If an organism feeds on something that made its own food, it is called a primary consumer. Many primary consumers are, in turn, eaten by other organisms, which are called secondary or tertiary (third level) consumers.

A simple **food chain** would be grass making its own food, which is eaten by a zebra, which is killed and eaten by a lion. Another example is grass, eaten by a field mouse, which is eaten by an owl. Still another example is plankton in the ocean, which is eaten by krill (a shrimp-like animal), and which is in turn eaten by a whale.

Not all relationships in nature are so simple. Instead, a **food web** may exist in which species are sometimes predators and sometimes prey. On the Arctic tundra, for example, caribou graze on lichens and plants. Summer mosquitoes feed by biting the caribou and other animals. Birds, in turn, eat the mosquitoes and other bugs. But birds may also become food for Arctic wolves. The wolves, in turn, might get bitten by mosquitoes or attacked by a polar bear.

How many of each type of organism is needed to maintain balance in nature? Generally, most areas support far fewer meat-eating animals (**carnivores**) than plant-eating animals (**herbivores**). In turn, each plant-eating animal needs many plants to support itself. As a result, scientists sometimes talk about a **food pyramid**. Organisms at the base of the pyramid support all the life forms above them.

CAUTION!

If you find a bat or any other mammal in the wild, do not handle it. A small number of these animals carry rabies, which is a deadly disease. If you are ever bitten or scratched by a bat or other wild animal, tell an adult immediately. They should call the local health department immediately. Rabies is a serious disease and you will need to be treated by a doctor to make sure you don't get the disease.

Bats

Living on every continent except Antarctica, bats use different adaptations to survive. For one thing, bats are **nocturnal**, or active at night. This **ecological niche** eliminates competition from animals that are active during the day.

As the only true flying mammals, bats can catch insects, snag treetop fruits, or sip flower nectar high off the ground. Bats' wings are really modified hands. Strong muscles between the wings' thin membranes power their flight.

Have you ever head the saying, "Blind as a bat"? In fact, contrary to popular legend, none of the 925 species of bats are blind. Large bats that feed on fruit often have very good eyesight. About 670 other bat species get help from **echolocation**. Think of it as an animal Marco Polo game. The difference is that the bat gets sounds back even when the prey don't want to play.

In echolocation, the bat gives a high-pitched cry. The cry is *ultrasonic*. That means its sound frequency is above the range people can hear. Then the bat listens. Returning echoes bouncing off of nearby objects tell the bat where food is.

Bats in warm climates are active year round. In colder areas, some bats like the Indiana bat hibernate in caves. They become inactive and let their body temperatures drop. Meanwhile, their bodies burn stored fat. Hibernation is an important adaptation for these bats and various other animals. It saves energy the animal would otherwise use keeping warm and searching for scarce food.

Vampire stories suggest that bats are blood suckers. Only three species of bats suck blood. They live in tropical or semi-tropical areas, and they feed on animals, not people.

Bats play important roles in nature. Many bats control pests by eating insects or other small animals. Still other bats eat fruit. They help spread seeds. Some may carry the fruit away from the tree before eating it, and then leave the seeds in the new spot. Others may actually eat the seeds with the fruit, but later pass them, unharmed, with their waste.

People often pose threats to bats. Pesticides can poison bats. Bats disturbed from hibernation may use up energy too quickly before spring comes. Building or mining projects can ruin bat homes.

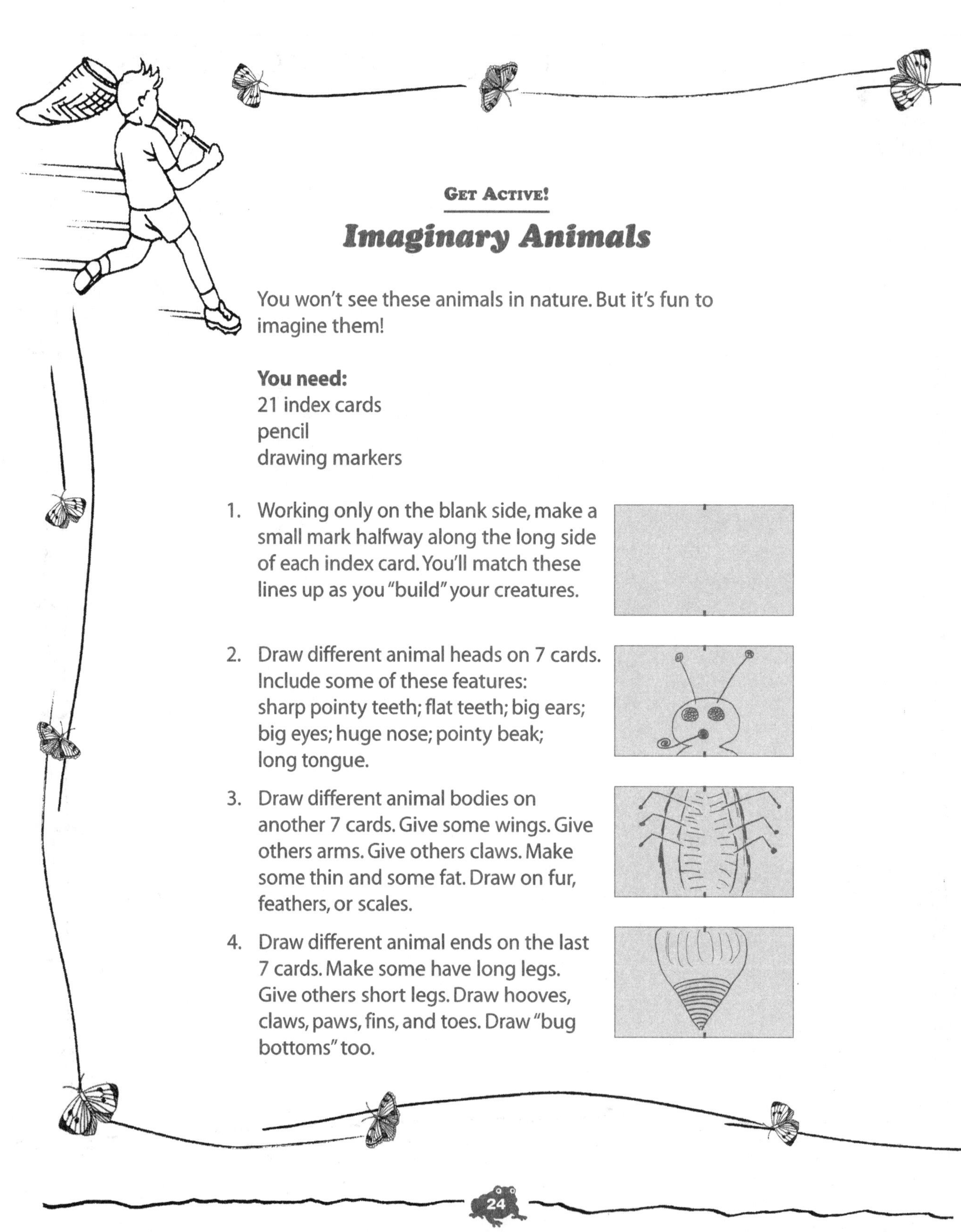

GET ACTIVE!

Imaginary Animals

You won't see these animals in nature. But it's fun to imagine them!

You need:
21 index cards
pencil
drawing markers

1. Working only on the blank side, make a small mark halfway along the long side of each index card. You'll match these lines up as you "build" your creatures.
2. Draw different animal heads on 7 cards. Include some of these features: sharp pointy teeth; flat teeth; big ears; big eyes; huge nose; pointy beak; long tongue.
3. Draw different animal bodies on another 7 cards. Give some wings. Give others arms. Give others claws. Make some thin and some fat. Draw on fur, feathers, or scales.
4. Draw different animal ends on the last 7 cards. Make some have long legs. Give others short legs. Draw hooves, claws, paws, fins, and toes. Draw "bug bottoms" too.

5. Now mix and match the cards to create imaginary animals. Make up stories about how different body parts help your animal survive in its habitat.

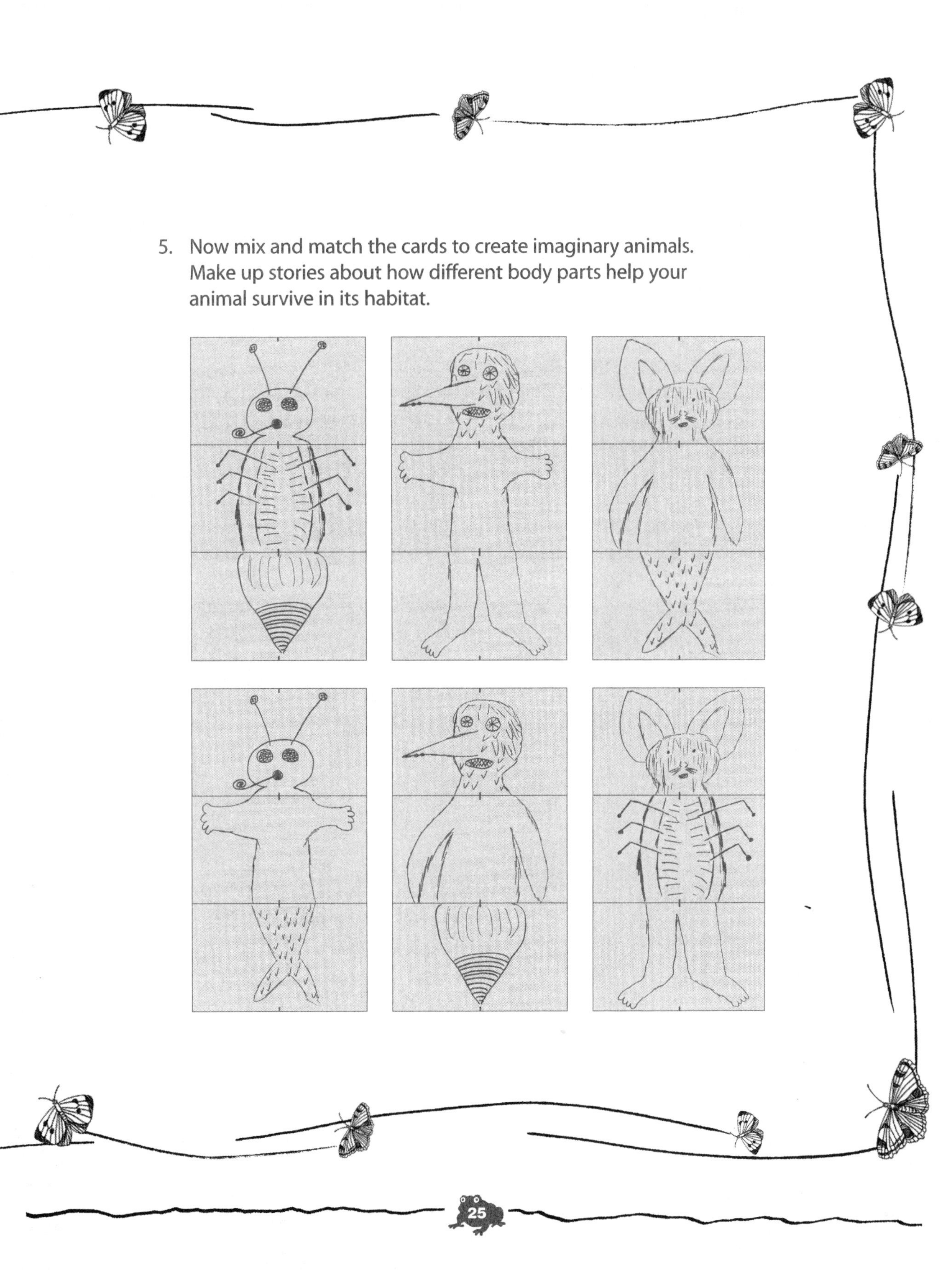

ADAPTED TO THE ENVIRONMENT

Surviving in nature can be tough, but organisms manage, thanks to adaptations. **Adaptations** are features that help life forms survive in their habitats, or homes.

Physical adaptations are part of the organism itself. Hummingbirds, for example, have thin, pointed beaks. The shape is just right for sucking nectar from trumpet-shaped flowers.

Spider monkeys' strong tails can support them as they hang from tree branches. The adaptation helps them find food and get around in the rain forest treetops.

adaptation: feature that helps a species survive in its environment. [ad-ap-TAY-shun]

Life forms may also make behavioral adaptations. In suburban areas near woods, for example, raccoons often "hunt" in garbage cans. Although buildings reduced their traditional habitat, they are still able to find food.

As you learn about nature's life forms, think about how they adapt to their environments. Nature's creatures are truly amazing.

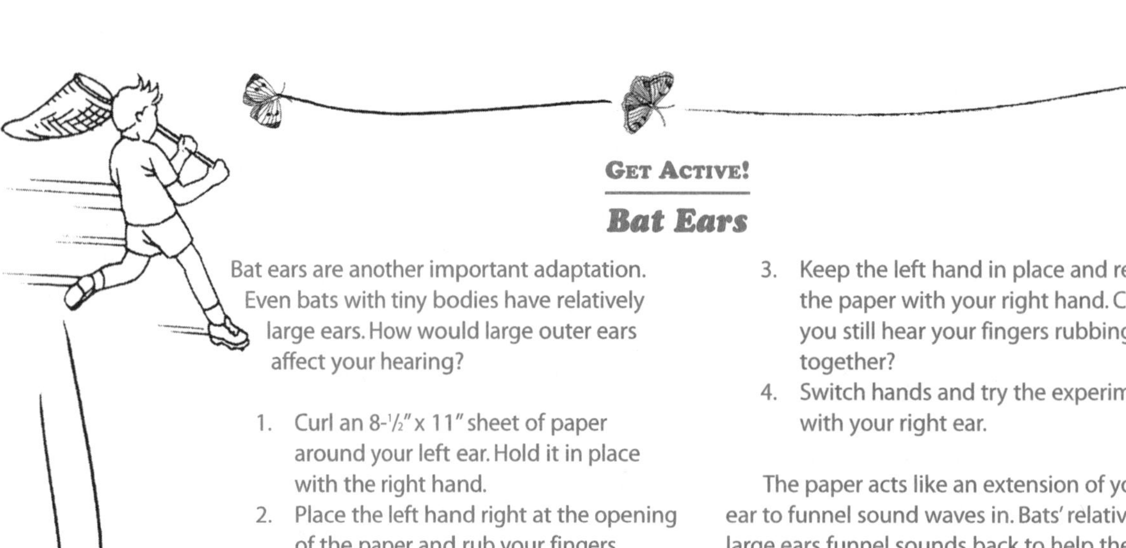

GET ACTIVE!

Bat Ears

Bat ears are another important adaptation. Even bats with tiny bodies have relatively large ears. How would large outer ears affect your hearing?

1. Curl an 8-½" x 11" sheet of paper around your left ear. Hold it in place with the right hand.
2. Place the left hand right at the opening of the paper and rub your fingers together. Can you hear the noise?
3. Keep the left hand in place and remove the paper with your right hand. Can you still hear your fingers rubbing together?
4. Switch hands and try the experiment with your right ear.

The paper acts like an extension of your ear to funnel sound waves in. Bats' relatively large ears funnel sounds back to help them find prey with echolocation.

CHAPTER 3
LIFE IN THE FOREST

CONIFEROUS FORESTS

Coniferous forests are filled with cone-bearing trees. Pine trees, for example, have pinecones. Cone-bearing trees are also found sometimes in "mixed forests" with other trees. But in cold climates and at high altitudes, only these evergreen trees can survive the harsh, cold winters.

coniferous: cone-bearing. [koh-NIFF-er-us]

deciduous: describes a plant that seasonally loses its leaves. [dee-SID-yoo-us]

What do cones do? They let the tree reproduce. Some cones release pollen. The wind carries the pollen away. If the pollen lands on a seed cone, it produces a sperm cell. When sperm joins with an egg cell inside the seed cone, a new plant grows.

Most cone-bearing trees are evergreens. They keep their smooth, waxy needle leaves year round. Needles hold water in very well. This especially helps during winter, when water in the ground may freeze.

While evergreen trees stay green year round, some of their needles do fall as trees grow or die. Thus, dry, brown needles often cover the floor of a coniferous forest, providing a home for insects.

TEMPERATE FORESTS

Temperate forests (also called broad-leafed forests) have mostly **deciduous** trees. As cool weather approaches, the tree stops sending water up to its leaves. As green chlorophyll fades away, the leaves turn yellow, orange, red, or brown. Finally, the dried leaves fall to the ground.

Fallen leaves do more than just crunch underfoot. They return important nutrients to the forest floor. These nutrients support fungi, insects, plants, and animals that make the forest their home.

Falling leaves help trees survive too. Freezing winter temperatures can keep water from flowing into roots and up tree trunks. During their dormant winter stage, however, the trees need very little water. When spring comes, new leaf buds burst forth. The yearly cycle starts again.

The forest is a dynamic place because of its cycle of sparse spring growth, heavy summer foliage, falling leaves, and bare winter branches. Each season presents a different view of nature.

ANATOMY OF A TREE

Forests, by definition, have trees. Do you know the parts of a tree?

Leaves are the tree's food factories. Like all green plants, they use chlorophyll to make sugar from water and carbon dioxide. Energy from sunlight powers the process.

At the bottom end are the tree's roots. *Roots* anchor the tree in the soil. They also soak up water for the leaves' photosynthesis.

The *trunk* is the tree's main stem. Smaller stems, called branches, grow out from the trunk. The trunk and branches support the tree. They also function as the tree's inner transport system.

GET ACTIVE!

Pine Cone Critter

You won't find this critter crawling around in nature. But it's fun to make this nature craft.

You need:

1 pine cone
wobbly glue-on eyes
brown or black felt
small pompom
scissors
glue

1. Fold felt in half and cut two paw-shaped pieces. Glue the paws to the pine cone so they stick out at the bottom.
2. Glue wobbly eyes on the top third of the pine cone.
3. Make ears and front paws for your critter. Fold the felt in half before cutting so your ears and paws match. Glue them in place.
4. Glue the pom pom to the pine cone for a tail.
5. Name your pine cone critter. Imagine where it would live in the forest if it were a real animal.

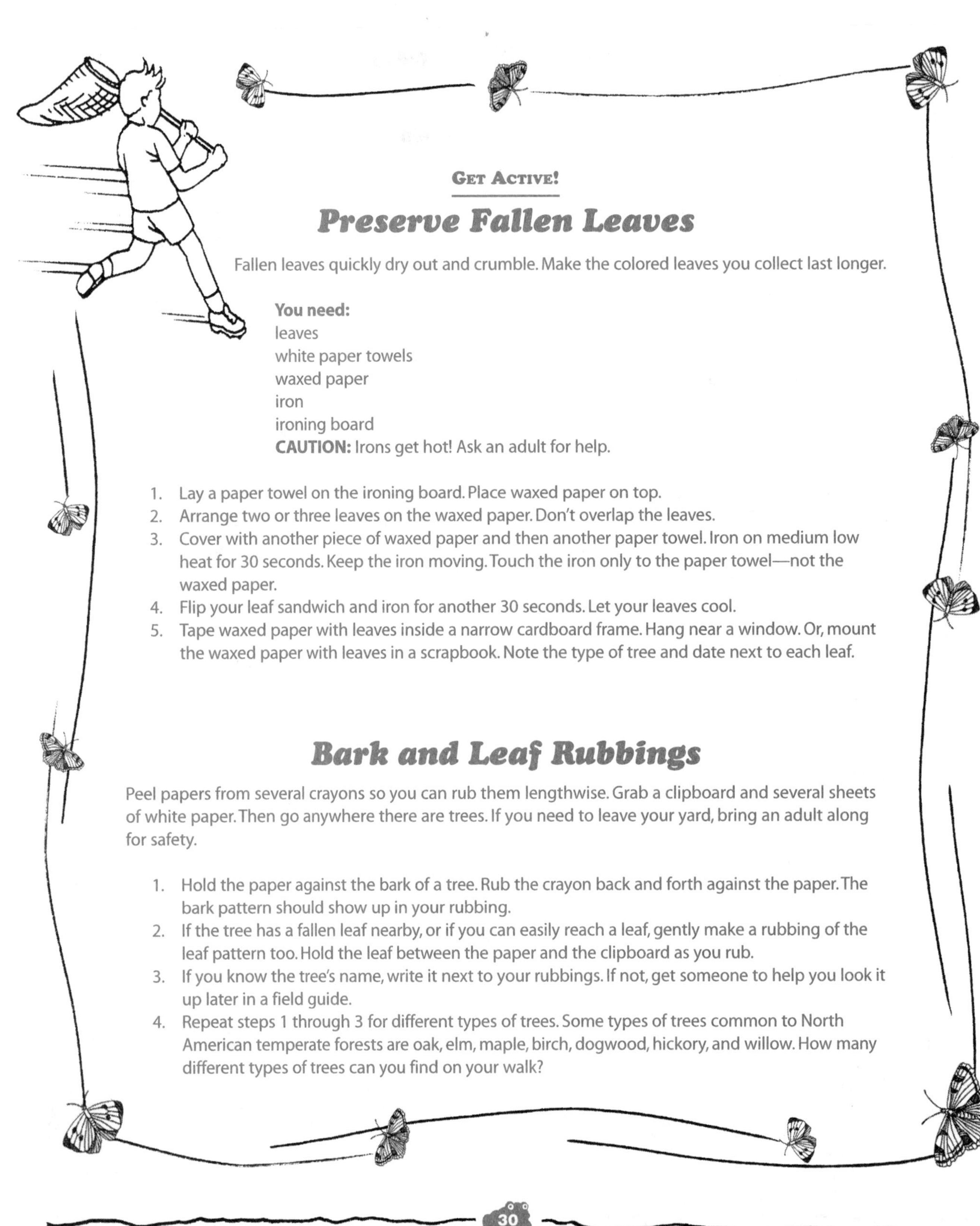

Get Active!

Preserve Fallen Leaves

Fallen leaves quickly dry out and crumble. Make the colored leaves you collect last longer.

You need:
leaves
white paper towels
waxed paper
iron
ironing board
CAUTION: Irons get hot! Ask an adult for help.

1. Lay a paper towel on the ironing board. Place waxed paper on top.
2. Arrange two or three leaves on the waxed paper. Don't overlap the leaves.
3. Cover with another piece of waxed paper and then another paper towel. Iron on medium low heat for 30 seconds. Keep the iron moving. Touch the iron only to the paper towel—not the waxed paper.
4. Flip your leaf sandwich and iron for another 30 seconds. Let your leaves cool.
5. Tape waxed paper with leaves inside a narrow cardboard frame. Hang near a window. Or, mount the waxed paper with leaves in a scrapbook. Note the type of tree and date next to each leaf.

Bark and Leaf Rubbings

Peel papers from several crayons so you can rub them lengthwise. Grab a clipboard and several sheets of white paper. Then go anywhere there are trees. If you need to leave your yard, bring an adult along for safety.

1. Hold the paper against the bark of a tree. Rub the crayon back and forth against the paper. The bark pattern should show up in your rubbing.
2. If the tree has a fallen leaf nearby, or if you can easily reach a leaf, gently make a rubbing of the leaf pattern too. Hold the leaf between the paper and the clipboard as you rub.
3. If you know the tree's name, write it next to your rubbings. If not, get someone to help you look it up later in a field guide.
4. Repeat steps 1 through 3 for different types of trees. Some types of trees common to North American temperate forests are oak, elm, maple, birch, dogwood, hickory, and willow. How many different types of trees can you find on your walk?

Inside the trunk are channels called **xylem** and **phloem**. Xylem rings on the trunk's inner part bring water from the roots up to the branches and leaves. Scientists estimate the age of most trees by counting the rings of xylem, one for each year of the tree's life.

Phloem tubes circle the tree outside the xylem rings. Phloem carries food from the leaves down to the rest of the plant.

Bark forms the trunk's outer protective layer. Don't carve your initials in tree bark, or you may expose cells underneath to disease and pests.

WORDS to KNOW

xylem: vascular tubes in tree trunk that carry water from the roots through the rest of the plant. [ZYE-lem]

phloem: vascular tubes in a tree trunk that bring food to the rest of the plant. [FLOW-em]

bark: outer covering of a tree.

MOSS ON THE FOREST FLOOR

Like a soft, green carpet, moss covers rocks and other areas in the temperate forest. But it's best not to walk on this carpet. It gets slippery.

Mosses are green plants. They need lots of moisture, so they usually grow in shady areas that stay wet.

Unlike ferns or flowering plants, mosses don't have vascular tubes. They can't move water up any great distance. As a result, mosses are usually 8 inches (20 cm) or shorter. Despite this limit, about 10,000 species of moss thrive worldwide. Look for moss when you walk through the forest.

IT'S A NATURAL FACT!

Habitat Means Home

Habitats are areas where living things make their homes. Temperature, rainfall, and other factors produce a variety of habitats. Each habitat plays an important part in the world of nature. Forest, grasslands, deserts, tundra, and watery areas are some of nature's most fascinating habitats.

THE DOUBLE LIFE OF FERNS

Leafy green ferns lead a double life. Feathery roots branch into the soil from a root-stock (trunk) or rhizome (horizontal stalk). The roots anchor the fern and absorb water from the soil. Stalks push up from the rootstock.

IT'S A NATURAL FACT!

Camouflage: Hiding in Plain Sight

Why are squirrels, chipmunks, groundhogs, deer, and other forest creatures often gray or brown? The drab coloring blends in with the forest.

Physical features that help animals hide are called camouflage. Camouflage protects them from danger. Others, like the lynx, use camouflage to hide from the animals they stalk.

Some animals change color. The snowshoe hare, for example, is brown in summer but turns white for the winter so it blends in with its snowy environment. The gecko, which lives in tropical climates, can change color to match its background.

Shape helps with camouflage too. A walking stick insect looks just like a tiny twig.

Don't worry if you don't always see wildlife on your nature walks. Camouflage may be hiding the animals!

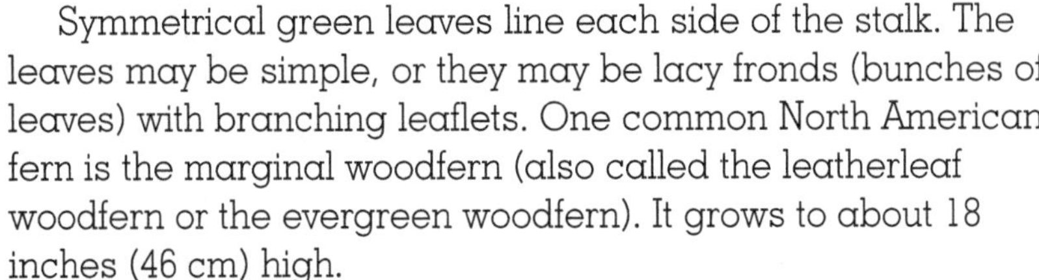

Symmetrical green leaves line each side of the stalk. The leaves may be simple, or they may be lacy fronds (bunches of leaves) with branching leaflets. One common North American fern is the marginal woodfern (also called the leatherleaf woodfern or the evergreen woodfern). It grows to about 18 inches (46 cm) high.

Don't wait for ferns to have flowers. It won't happen because ferns don't reproduce that way. Instead, come late summer, the marginal woodfern develops rust-colored fruitdots on the underside of some leaves. Spores grow inside these dots.

On a dry, windy day, the fern's fruitdots burst open. Spores shoot into the air, where the wind bears them away.

When a spore lands in a moist, shady spot, it starts growing. Instead of something like the original fern, a green, heart-shaped cushion grows. Less than an inch (2.5 cm) big, it is the **gametophyte** stage of the fern's life. (Mosses and certain other plants have gametophyte stages too.)

The plant's sexual structures develop on the cushion's underside. You can't see them without a microscope. Sperm from the male structures swim toward female structures at the cushion's notched end. When an egg is fertilized, it starts developing.

Now a root grows down into the soil, and a stem grows upward. Soon, the new plant looks like the original fern.

Biologists call this cycle "alternation of generations." Both stages are essential to the species' survival.

FOREST FLOWERS

Many wildflowers bloom in spring before tree leaves shade the forest floor. Bluebells bloom with their pretty blue flowers. Jack-in-the-pulpit's greenish-brown flowers stand like little vases. Lily-of-the-valley's tiny white blossoms drape gracefully amid leaves that look like

gametophyte: the life stage of a fern resulting from asexual reproduction; other organisms have gametophyte stages too. [ga-MET-oh-fite]

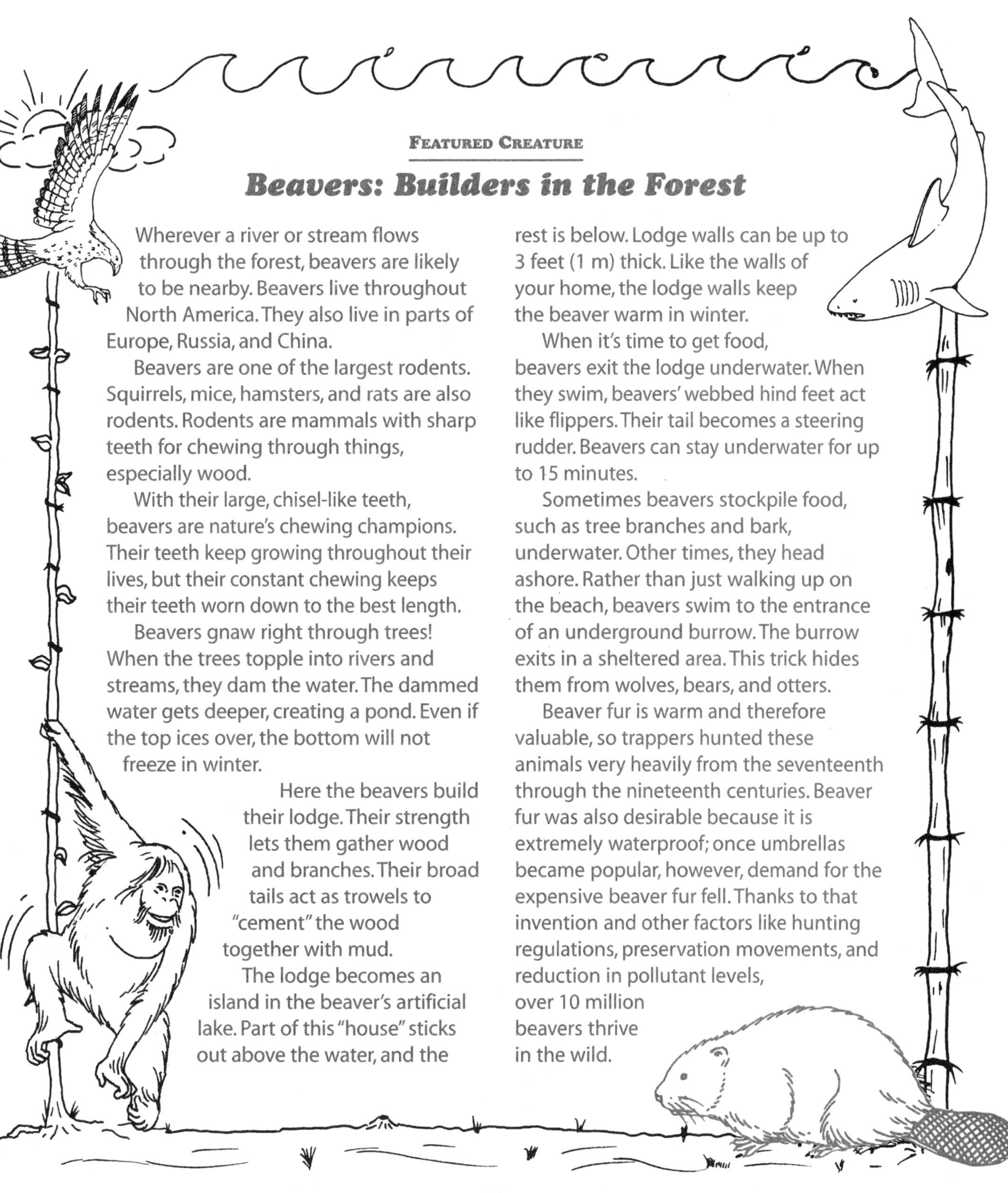

Featured Creature

Beavers: Builders in the Forest

Wherever a river or stream flows through the forest, beavers are likely to be nearby. Beavers live throughout North America. They also live in parts of Europe, Russia, and China.

Beavers are one of the largest rodents. Squirrels, mice, hamsters, and rats are also rodents. Rodents are mammals with sharp teeth for chewing through things, especially wood.

With their large, chisel-like teeth, beavers are nature's chewing champions. Their teeth keep growing throughout their lives, but their constant chewing keeps their teeth worn down to the best length.

Beavers gnaw right through trees! When the trees topple into rivers and streams, they dam the water. The dammed water gets deeper, creating a pond. Even if the top ices over, the bottom will not freeze in winter.

Here the beavers build their lodge. Their strength lets them gather wood and branches. Their broad tails act as trowels to "cement" the wood together with mud.

The lodge becomes an island in the beaver's artificial lake. Part of this "house" sticks out above the water, and the rest is below. Lodge walls can be up to 3 feet (1 m) thick. Like the walls of your home, the lodge walls keep the beaver warm in winter.

When it's time to get food, beavers exit the lodge underwater. When they swim, beavers' webbed hind feet act like flippers. Their tail becomes a steering rudder. Beavers can stay underwater for up to 15 minutes.

Sometimes beavers stockpile food, such as tree branches and bark, underwater. Other times, they head ashore. Rather than just walking up on the beach, beavers swim to the entrance of an underground burrow. The burrow exits in a sheltered area. This trick hides them from wolves, bears, and otters.

Beaver fur is warm and therefore valuable, so trappers hunted these animals very heavily from the seventeenth through the nineteenth centuries. Beaver fur was also desirable because it is extremely waterproof; once umbrellas became popular, however, demand for the expensive beaver fur fell. Thanks to that invention and other factors like hunting regulations, preservation movements, and reduction in pollutant levels, over 10 million beavers thrive in the wild.

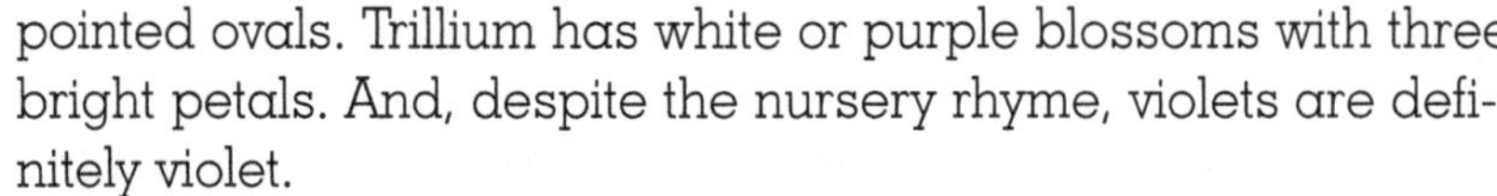

IT'S A NATURAL FACT!

Don't Be Fooled by Cartoon Characters

Cartoons sometimes show characters cuddling up with raccoons, mice, rabbits, squirrels, or other wild animals. You can enjoy watching these and other animals in nature, but NEVER try to cuddle or pet a wild animal like you see in the cartoons.

Wild animals may bite or scratch. You might even catch diseases from certain animals.

You might unknowingly hurt the animal too. Some animal mothers won't care for their babies if they detect a human smell on them.

If you find an injured animal in the woods or elsewhere, leave it alone, but note the location. Then call your local park ranger's office, animal rehabilitation center, or board of health. They will do anything that needs to be done.

pointed ovals. Trillium has white or purple blossoms with three bright petals. And, despite the nursery rhyme, violets are definitely violet.

Other flowers bloom during summer. They enjoy the cooling shade provided by the trees' leaves. Honeysuckle, for example, gives off a pleasant sweet scent in midsummer.

SMELLS AND SPINES

What's that foul smell? It could be a skunk.

Skunks live in both forests and grasslands. These black mammals with a white stripe down their backs and tails are mostly active at night. They may look cute, but if you see one, back away carefully. Skunks give off an awful odor when enemies come near. It's really hard to wash the terrible smell away.

Don't bother a porcupine either. Sharp quills cover this rodent's neck, back, and tail. The quills are modified hairs.

If a porcupine feels threatened, it releases some of its quills. Sharp barbs at the end of the tips dig into the porcupine's attacker. The attacker backs away in pain, while the porcupine scurries to safety. And contrary to popular legend, porcupines cannot "throw" their quills great distances—you do have to touch them to get stuck with their quills, but not very hard. Many dogs find this out to their painful dismay!

The hedgehog uses a different strategy. Using muscles on its back, it rolls itself up and tucks its head and paws inside. Now it looks like a ball of brown needles. These sharp spines keep most predators away. When danger is over, the hedgehog cautiously peeks out. After pushing out its head, the hedgehog flips over to push out all four paws. This protects its soft furry underside in case danger comes back.

Hedgehogs live in Europe, Asia, and Africa. The Western European hedgehog's preferred habitat is temperate forests. It also lives in bushy areas and parks where leaves fall. Leaves make a comfortable nest. Leaves also hold lots of insects, a favorite meal for the hedgehog.

Besides insects, hedgehogs feast on snails, worms, and even vipers. Sometimes hedgehogs eat fruit too. If a hedgehog rolls on top of a small piece of fruit, the fruit sticks to its spines. Then the hedgehog can carry the fruit to its nest for dessert.

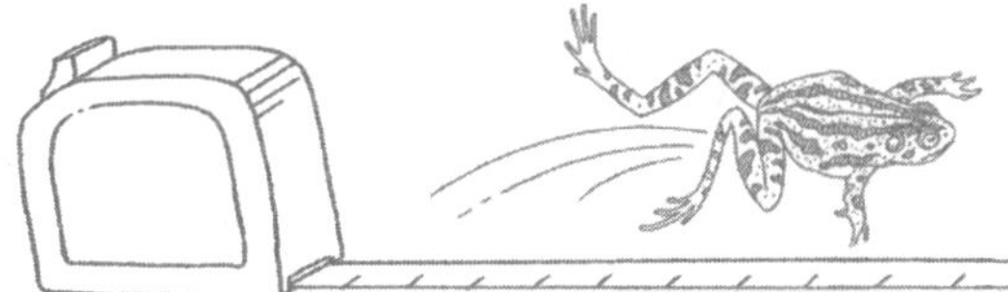

NATURE STATS

Flower Power

Scientists have discovered about 250,000 different species of flowering plants throughout the world. Flowers function to let the plant reproduce. Male sex cells from pollen travel down a tube to fertilize the female sex cells, or ova, to form seeds. The seeds can later grow to form a new plant.

GET ACTIVE!

Forest Scavenger Hunt

Challenge your friends to a forest scavenger hunt. Be sure adults come along for safety.

1. Divide your group into two or three teams. Make sure each team has at least two people.
2. Each team gets the same list of items to spot on a forest walk. Possible items to include on the list are: pine cone, pine needles, fern, moss, wildflower, oak leaf, elm leaf, ash leaf, maple leaf, vine, berry, mud, large rocks, fallen tree, bird's nest, squirrel, deer, chipmunk, bird, spider, spider web, stream.
3. Teams divide up and walk through the woods. Keep together and stay on paths. If you see any wildlife along the trail, try not to bother it.
4. When a team spots an item on the list, each member marks the time it was seen.
5. After half an hour, teams meet back at an agreed-upon spot and compare lists. The team that spotted the most list items wins.

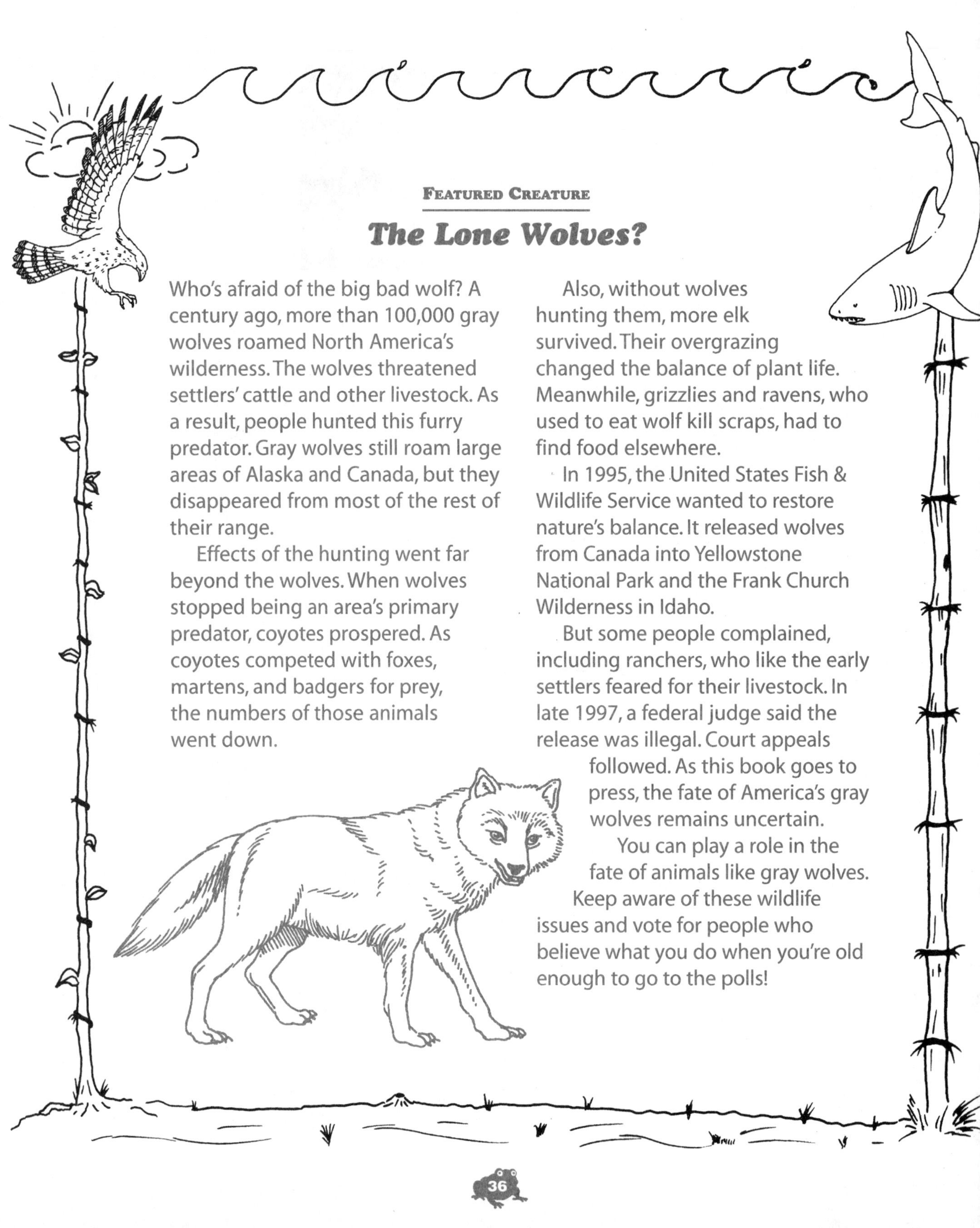

FEATURED CREATURE

The Lone Wolves?

Who's afraid of the big bad wolf? A century ago, more than 100,000 gray wolves roamed North America's wilderness. The wolves threatened settlers' cattle and other livestock. As a result, people hunted this furry predator. Gray wolves still roam large areas of Alaska and Canada, but they disappeared from most of the rest of their range.

Effects of the hunting went far beyond the wolves. When wolves stopped being an area's primary predator, coyotes prospered. As coyotes competed with foxes, martens, and badgers for prey, the numbers of those animals went down.

Also, without wolves hunting them, more elk survived. Their overgrazing changed the balance of plant life. Meanwhile, grizzlies and ravens, who used to eat wolf kill scraps, had to find food elsewhere.

In 1995, the United States Fish & Wildlife Service wanted to restore nature's balance. It released wolves from Canada into Yellowstone National Park and the Frank Church Wilderness in Idaho.

But some people complained, including ranchers, who like the early settlers feared for their livestock. In late 1997, a federal judge said the release was illegal. Court appeals followed. As this book goes to press, the fate of America's gray wolves remains uncertain.

You can play a role in the fate of animals like gray wolves. Keep aware of these wildlife issues and vote for people who believe what you do when you're old enough to go to the polls!

CHAPTER 4
TROPICAL RAIN FORESTS

WARM AND WET

Lush tropical rain forests provide a home to at least half the species on Earth. Located in tropical areas, rain forests get nearly even amounts of light and dark every day throughout the year. Year-round average temperatures range from 73°F (23°C) to 87°F (31°C).

As the name implies, rain forests get lots of rain—usually at least 80 inches (200 cm) or more per year. In some areas, torrential monsoons dump enormous amounts of water during the rainy season. Cherrapunji, India, got over 1,000 inches (2,600 cm) of rain one year! Farther east, heavy summer rains swell Cambodia's Tonle Sap, or Great Lake, up to 10 times its winter size.

Other rain forest areas get more consistent rainfall through the year. Even then, it may rain almost every day. Climb to the top of Hawaii's extinct Diamond Head volcano just as an afternoon rain ends, and you'll likely see a beautiful rainbow!

LOTS OF LIFE FROM BOTTOM TO TOP

City apartment buildings let lots of people live on a small area of land. Likewise, rain forests house many different life forms in each of their layers.

Shadowed by taller trees and vines, the rain forest **floor**

WORDS to KNOW

floor: when used in connection with the rain forest, the lowest layer at which living things thrive.

understory: layer of the rain forest above the floor and beneath the canopy.

GET ACTIVE!

Grow a Rain Forest Plant

Many popular houseplants are rain forest natives. Adapted to the semi-dark rain forest floor and understory, they grow well in indirect indoor light.

Buy a small rain forest plant from a nearby nursery. You may want to try an African violet or leafy green spathiphyllum. If you're more ambitious, try a bromeliad or ficus tree. Or ask the nursery salesperson for recommendations.

Water your plant regularly. Keep the soil damp to the touch, but not soaking. Be sure the pot has drainage and a saucer underneath. You might want to buy a mister—an inexpensive plastic spray bottle will do or recycle an old window cleaner bottle if you rinse it out well. Some tropical plants, especially those with shiny leaves, enjoy the mist. It simulates the rain forest environment. Enjoy your plant!

is semi-dark and damp. Warm humidity encourages quick decay of fallen leaves and other debris with the help of fungi and bacteria. Ferns and small plants with broad leaves soak up the little sunlight reaching the floor. Tree saplings start growing upward toward the light.

Ants, termites, and other insects thrive on the forest floor. Mammals such as gorillas, tapirs, and capybaras graze along the ground. And a whole host of fishes, reptiles, and other animals live in and by the rivers that flow through the rain forest.

The **understory** reaches from the forest floor up to about 60 feet (18 m). Vines and other plants anchor themselves among the trees. Margeys and ocelots prowl in the branches, while birds search for insect meals.

Still higher is the **canopy**, reaching from 60 to 120 feet (26 m) above the ground. Like a tent, tree leaves and branches form a canopy, or roof, over the rain forest's lower layers. Abundant sunlight encourages bromeliads and other flowers to grow on the branches.

Parrots, toucans, and other birds squawk loudly to each other from the treetops. Hummingbirds sip from orchids. Howler monkeys, chimpanzees, orangutans, anteaters, bats, and sloths also make their homes high in the treetops.

Rising above the canopy to about 200 feet (60 m) is the **emergent layer**. A few tall trees grow in this layer, soaking up bright sunlight in the brisk winds.

WORDS to KNOW

canopy: layer of the rain forest near the top of most trees. [CAN-oh-pee]

emergent layer: vertical layer of the rain forest that only the tallest trees reach. [ee-MERJ-ent LAY-er]

DIVERSITY IN THE RAIN FOREST

How many types of organisms live on Earth? Scientists don't yet know.

"The estimate of total number of species in the world ranges from about 10 million to 30 million," says F. Lynn Carpenter, an Ecology Professor at the University of California at Irvine. So far, scientists have described only about 2 million of those species. Many more are waiting to be discovered. "Most of these occur in the rain forest," says Carpenter.

While tropical rain forests cover only 8 percent of Earth's surface, over half of all species find homes there. The Amazon of South America, the world's largest rain forest, has 80,000 species of plants. New England, in contrast, has only 1,200.

Peru's rain forests have 153 species of bats. That's more than three times the total number of bat species found in Canada and the United States. While

IT'S A NATURAL FACT!

Relying on Each Other

Plants and animals often rely on each other for survival. If lemurs disappeared from Madagascar, twenty types of trees could disappear. The lemurs eat fruit from the trees and help spread their seeds.

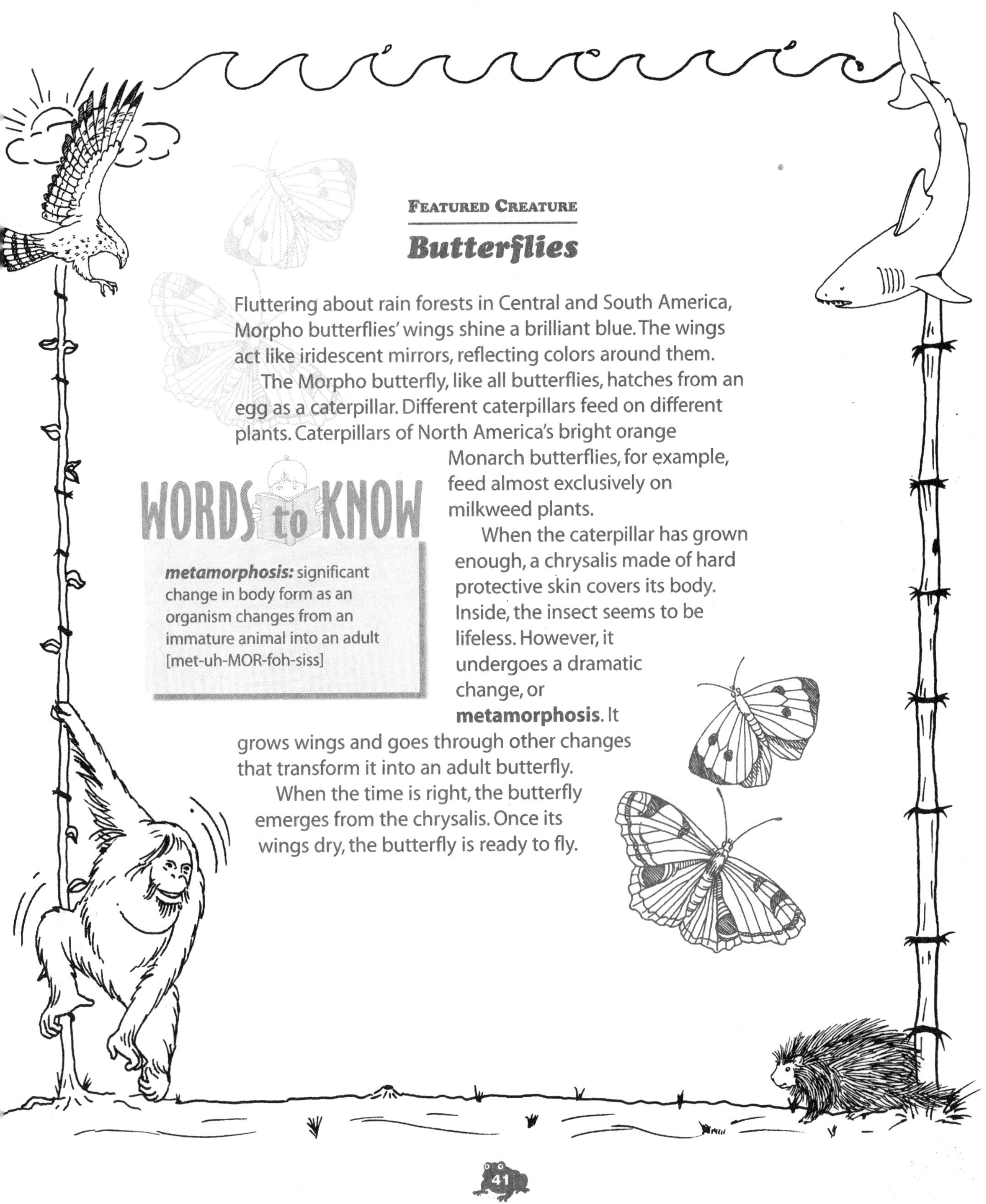

FEATURED CREATURE

Butterflies

Fluttering about rain forests in Central and South America, Morpho butterflies' wings shine a brilliant blue. The wings act like iridescent mirrors, reflecting colors around them.

The Morpho butterfly, like all butterflies, hatches from an egg as a caterpillar. Different caterpillars feed on different plants. Caterpillars of North America's bright orange Monarch butterflies, for example, feed almost exclusively on milkweed plants.

When the caterpillar has grown enough, a chrysalis made of hard protective skin covers its body. Inside, the insect seems to be lifeless. However, it undergoes a dramatic change, or **metamorphosis**. It grows wings and goes through other changes that transform it into an adult butterfly.

When the time is right, the butterfly emerges from the chrysalis. Once its wings dry, the butterfly is ready to fly.

WORDS to KNOW

metamorphosis: significant change in body form as an organism changes from an immature animal into an adult [met-uh-MOR-foh-siss]

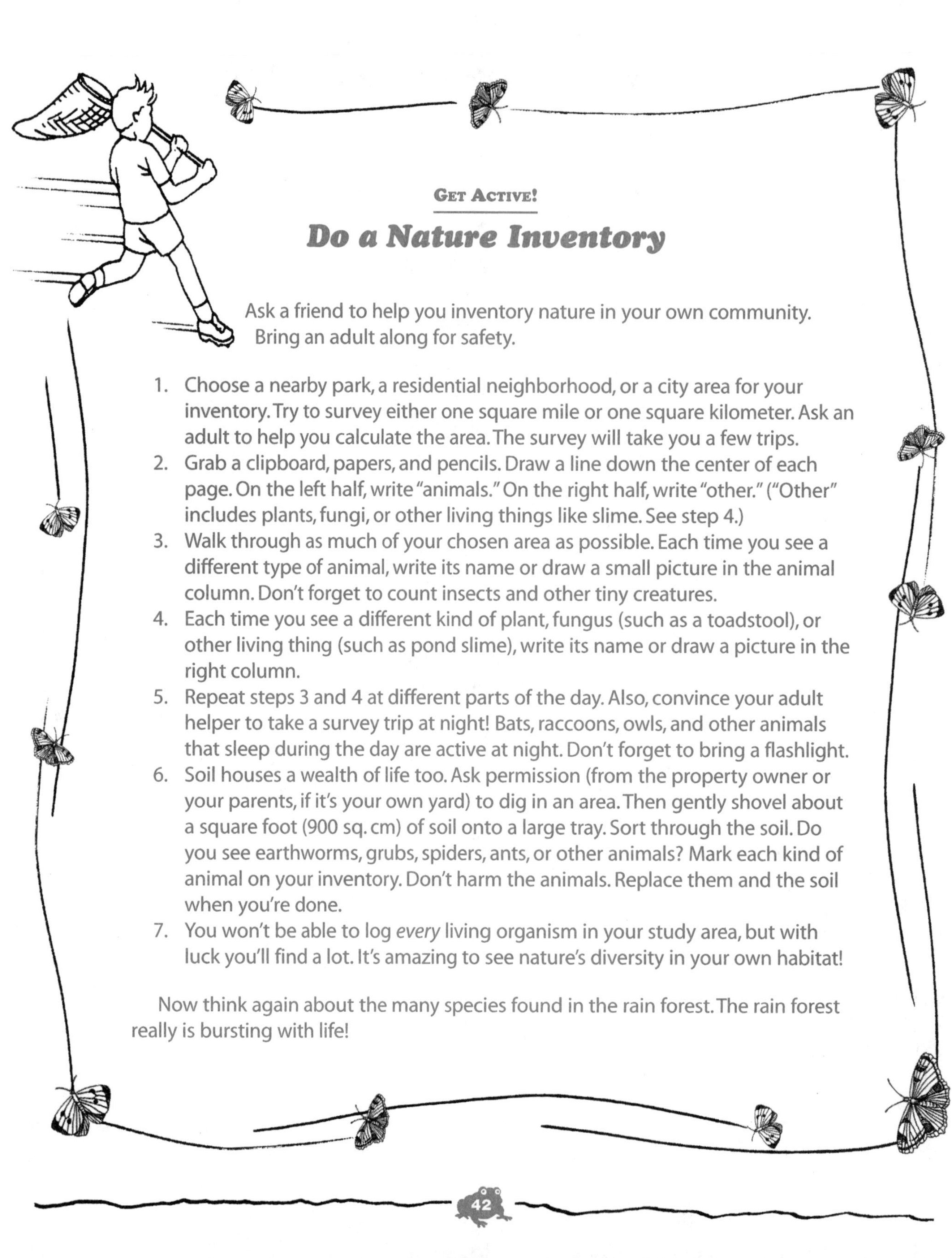

GET ACTIVE!

Do a Nature Inventory

Ask a friend to help you inventory nature in your own community. Bring an adult along for safety.

1. Choose a nearby park, a residential neighborhood, or a city area for your inventory. Try to survey either one square mile or one square kilometer. Ask an adult to help you calculate the area. The survey will take you a few trips.
2. Grab a clipboard, papers, and pencils. Draw a line down the center of each page. On the left half, write "animals." On the right half, write "other." ("Other" includes plants, fungi, or other living things like slime. See step 4.)
3. Walk through as much of your chosen area as possible. Each time you see a different type of animal, write its name or draw a small picture in the animal column. Don't forget to count insects and other tiny creatures.
4. Each time you see a different kind of plant, fungus (such as a toadstool), or other living thing (such as pond slime), write its name or draw a picture in the right column.
5. Repeat steps 3 and 4 at different parts of the day. Also, convince your adult helper to take a survey trip at night! Bats, raccoons, owls, and other animals that sleep during the day are active at night. Don't forget to bring a flashlight.
6. Soil houses a wealth of life too. Ask permission (from the property owner or your parents, if it's your own yard) to dig in an area. Then gently shovel about a square foot (900 sq. cm) of soil onto a large tray. Sort through the soil. Do you see earthworms, grubs, spiders, ants, or other animals? Mark each kind of animal on your inventory. Don't harm the animals. Replace them and the soil when you're done.
7. You won't be able to log *every* living organism in your study area, but with luck you'll find a lot. It's amazing to see nature's diversity in your own habitat!

Now think again about the many species found in the rain forest. The rain forest really is bursting with life!

the United Kingdom has 1,450 species of seed plants, Malaysia's rain forests have 8,000 species on less than half the area.

Costa Rica alone has 1,500 species of trees, including 65 fig tree species. A different kind of wasp pollinates each fig tree species.

Costa Rica also has 366,000 arthropods. Arthropods include all sorts of insects, spiders, and crustaceans. Over 500 species of butterflies flutter about Costa Rica's Monteverde Cloud Forest. Among them is the iridescent blue Morpho butterfly.

Who knows what species scientists will discover next as they study nature's rain forests?

ANIMAL COMMUNICATION

We can't talk to the animals like Hugh Lofting's hero in *The Story of Dr. Doolittle*, but animals communicate with each other well enough. Some animals communicate with sound. Others use visual displays. Still others rely on smell or touch.

Just what are the animals "saying"? Both in the rain forest and in other natural habitats, animal messages fall in broad categories that get important information across about mating and survival.

"Won't You Be Mine?" Animals don't send valentines, but they do want to attract mates. So, they draw attention to themselves.

Male grasshoppers chirp by stroking their hind legs over their wings. Male fiddler crabs wave their huge claws. Fireflies light up parts of their abdomens on summer nights to form code-like patterns.

Male ruffs and other birds strut back and forth to show off their brightly colored feathers. Some

NATURE STATS

Fewer Rain Forests

It's hard to say just how much of Earth's tropical forests were destroyed during the twentieth century. But some of the estimates are startling:

- Over 200,000 square miles of the Amazon rain forest was destroyed from 1978 to 1996. Over 11,000 square miles were deforested just in 1995.
- From 1973 to 1985, Southeast Asia lost 14 percent of its forest cover. That's over 98 million hectares.

Hunting hurts too. Some scientists say up to 24 million animals are hunted and killed each year in the Amazon rain forest.

Featured Creature

Toucans

From toe to top, toucans are adapted to life in the rain forest. Toucan feet have four toes—all with strong claws. Two toes face forward, while the other two face backward. This design gives toucans a strong grip on rain forest tree branches.

Using their strong leg and feet muscles, toucans twist in almost every direction to reach fruit near their perches. Fruit is the mainstay of toucan diets. Sometimes they also eat insects, spiders, termites, and other small invertebrates.

Criss-crossed bits of bony material give toucans' big bony beaks maximum strength with minimum weight. Serrated edges let the beak easily cut through fruits.

Scientists think the beak's bright colors may help members of the approximately 40 toucan species identify each other. The Toco toucan has the biggest beak. At 8 inches (20 cm) long, it's one third of the toucan's total length.

To get food from the tip of the beak back into the throat, toucans jerk their heads back and open the beak. By eating fruit and berries from one area, and eliminating some seeds as waste in another, toucans help disperse seeds so new plants can grow.

Roosting on tree branches, toucans often look like a ball of feathers. They twist back their heads to lay their beaks on top of their backs. Then they tip their tails up to cover the bill and back. Maybe they are trying to hide the brightly colored beak while they are sleeping!

Toucans build nests in tree holes lined with wood debris or seed pellets. Females lay two to four eggs at a time. Then both parents take turns warming the eggs until they hatch.

Nestlings don't open their eyes until they are three weeks old. Their feathers take over a month to grow in. Not until about seven weeks after birth do the chicks fledge, or fly on their own. In the meantime, both parents bring them food.

Toucans live only in rain forests from southern Mexico through South America. Toucans and hundreds of other birds rely on the rain forest for their survival.

GET ACTIVE!

Firefly Flashes

Male and female fireflies flash to each other with a kind of insect code. The information helps them find mates.

Fireflies are out in force during July in many parts of the United States. Capture one or two of these insects in a jar with a lid just after dark. Then watch their flashy displays.

Use a stopwatch to time how long the firefly's abdomen stays lit. Also time how long it is between flashes.

When you're done, uncap the jar and let the insects fly away. Always treat all forms of wildlife with kindness and respect.

birds, like white gannets, preen each other. That means they help clean bugs and dirt out of their feathers. Still other birds, like grebes, seem to have mating dances. In a display called rushing, grebes look like they're running across the water's surface.

"I'm Tough." A male gorilla shows he's the boss with a threat display. The gorilla stands on his hind legs, beats his chest, and yanks at nearby branches. This behavior shows that the male holds senior rank in the band. It can also intimidate others who might challenge the gorilla. Male baboons show they're in charge by baring their teeth.

A ring-tailed lemur may walk with her long tail held high in the air. The signal shows her leadership role in the group.

"Don't Hassle With Me." If a tiger bares its teeth, wrinkles its nose, and sets its ears back, watch out. The tiger is ready to attack if necessary.

An aggressive look on a wolf's face can warn other wolves to leave it alone. On the other hand, a wolf with its tail between its legs says it doesn't want to challenge another wolf.

Rattlesnakes can bite attackers with their fangs, but then they can't attack prey to eat right away. They have to build up their venom supply first. So sometimes when they're threatened, rattlesnakes shake their rattles—a group of bony pieces at the end of their tails. The rattle noise warns off the rattlesnake's enemies.

"Watch Out!" While meerkats hunt and dig in southern Africa's deserts, at least

one member of the group keeps lookout. If danger comes near, the meerkat barks loudly. Its barking sends everyone rushing to their burrows.

Likewise, the Arctic ground squirrel's loud chirp tells others that an enemy lurks nearby. The sound sends everyone bolting for cover.

"Keep Out!" The Klipspringer antelope wipes scent from glands on its face against branches. The scent tells other antelopes to stay away from its territory.

Hippos and white rhinos use really smelly scent marking to define their territory. The white rhino sprays urine around. The hippo whirls its tail to fling dung over a wide area.

RAIN FORESTS AT RISK

Each year millions of acres of rain forest are burned or bulldozed. Some people want to plant crops. Others want to erect new buildings.

Once an area of rain forest is lost, it can't easily be restored. Without the native plants, rainwater runs off, washing away nutrients in the top soil layer. The natural balance is upset, and plants, fungi, and animals cannot easily reestablish themselves. Species that depended on the rain forest become threatened.

Deforestation has effects even beyond rain forest plants and animals. Medicines to treat malaria, leukemia, and many other diseases were first found in the rain forest.

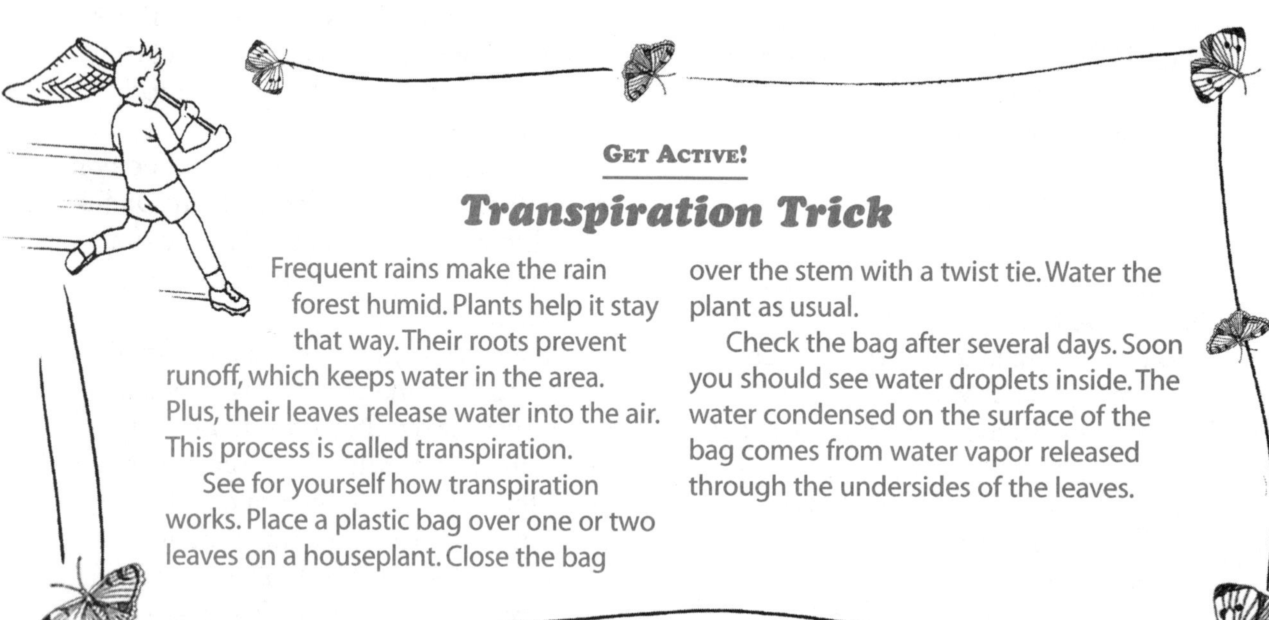

GET ACTIVE!

Transpiration Trick

Frequent rains make the rain forest humid. Plants help it stay that way. Their roots prevent runoff, which keeps water in the area. Plus, their leaves release water into the air. This process is called transpiration.

See for yourself how transpiration works. Place a plastic bag over one or two leaves on a houseplant. Close the bag over the stem with a twist tie. Water the plant as usual.

Check the bag after several days. Soon you should see water droplets inside. The water condensed on the surface of the bag comes from water vapor released through the undersides of the leaves.

What other cures could have come from species that lost their habitat?

Rain forests also help maintain balance in the atmosphere. Plants' photosynthesis takes in carbon dioxide from the air and releases oxygen. A lot of the carbon becomes part of the plants as they grow.

With fewer plants, Earth's level of carbon dioxide can rise. The result can be a gradual increase in world temperatures—also known as **global warming**. Over time, scientists believe global warming can cause more severe storms and other environmental problems.

But people are working to protect the rain forests. Some countries and groups set rain forest land aside as protected preserves. About 12 percent of Costa Rica's land now lies in national parks. Private parks, like the Monteverde Cloud Forest and the Bosque Eterno de los Niños (Children's Eternal Rain Forest), bring the amount of protected areas up to about 25 percent of the country's territory. Tax incentives, treaty provisions, and other programs encourage protection of even more land.

Ecotourism helps too. Instead of razing the rain forest for farming or logging, local people earn a living from tours, hotels, and other activities related to showing the rain forest to tourists.

Sustainable development is key. This means activities that can keep producing income. Instead of cutting an area of forest for a one-time profit of $1,000, for example, companies could pay local people to harvest products growing naturally in the area for $400 annually. Over 10 years, the total profit would be $4,000—much more than the one-time $1,000 payment. Plus, the area would still be productive for future years.

Even if you don't live in a rain forest, learn more about how to protect these natural areas. They play a vital role in Earth's global well-being.

WORDS to KNOW

global warming: gradual increase in Earth's overall average annual temperatures, believed to result from increasing concentrations of carbon dioxide and other "greenhouse gases" in the atmosphere.

sustainable development: economic growth that can continue to produce income year after year. [sus-TANE-uh-bul dee-VEL-up-ment]

CHAPTER 5
GRASSLANDS

WORDS to KNOW

monocot: category of plants that includes grasses. [MONN-oh-cot]

prairie: type of grassland found on the Great Plains of North America. [PRAY-ree]

PRAIRIES

Imagine a sea of tall grass stretching for miles and miles. Pioneers on the American frontier saw just that when they came to the Great Plains. Pioneers even called their covered wagons prairie schooners—as if they were indeed ships crossing an uncharted sea.

The Great Plains stretch over a thousand miles. They run from Alberta and Manitoba in Canada southward to Texas. Most of the Great Plains is flat, with few hills or mountains.

Today much of the Great Plains is used for farming. The soil and climate support wheat, rye, corn, and other crops, making this area known as America's "bread basket." Yet beautiful parks and natural areas still remain in the Great Plains and other grasslands.

LEAVES OF GRASS

As the name implies, grass is the dominant plant in grasslands. But grass is more than just green stuff to mow.

Look closely at a blade of grass. Ridges run up and down the blade. They don't branch out from a central spot like many bush, flowers, and tree leaves do. Grasses are a type of plant known as **monocots**.

Over 10,000 different species of grass live in different parts of the world.

NATURE STATS

Prairie Bird Numbers Dip Down

The North American Breeding Bird Survey says numbers of various grassland songbirds dipped from 1966 to 1996. Some examples:

Henslow's sparrow—down 93 percent
Sprague's pipit—down 75 percent
Grasshopper sparrow—down 66 percent

Scientists say land development—mostly for farming—has changed much of the grassland birds' natural habitats. Protecting these species is important. Otherwise future birdwatchers may not have much to see!

Featured Creature

Prairie Dogs

Prairie dogs live on the prairie and sound like barking dogs. But these 16-inch-tall (41 cm) mammals are not dogs. They belong to the squirrel family.

Prairie dogs dig burrows for their homes. Just as many houses have a front door and a back door, prairie dogs build burrows with multiple entrances. If a ferret, coyote, or bobcat waits at one end, the prairie dog escapes from another opening.

Prairie dog burrows are more than just tunnels. They have little chambers, or rooms. One chamber may be a nursery for baby prairie dogs. Another may serve as a prairie dog bedroom.

Prairie dogs are very social animals. When they meet, they sniff each other's faces. Other times prairie dogs play wrestle. Prairie dogs also take turns cleaning fleas or other pests from each other's fur.

Prairie dog colonies or towns can have more than 100 members. Large colonies provide protection. While most group members feed on grass, roots, or seeds, some act as sentries. If danger approaches, the sentries chirp loudly. The noise warns the group to rush quickly back to the burrow.

For many years, farmers on the Great Plains hated prairie dogs. They worried that prairie dogs would eat their crops. They also feared that cattle would trip over burrow entrances. To get rid of prairie dogs, farmers used poison, smoke bombs, guns, and even flooding.

Prairie dog numbers have dropped dramatically. Once North America had over 5 billion black-tailed prairie dogs. By 1999, only about 10 million remained. As this book goes to press, the United States government is considering whether to protect prairie dogs under the Endangered Species Act.

steppe: dry grassland, such as that found in eastern Europe and western Asia.

savanna: type of grassland where coarse grasses grow in patches, such as that found in tropical Africa. [suh-VAN-uh]

forb: catch-all phrase for plants that aren't trees or bushes; the term includes plants such as herbs and wildflowers.

Tall-grass **prairies** get enough rainfall to grow grasses several feet high. Wheat, oats, corn, and rye are all tall grasses.

Mixed-grass prairies support both tall and short grasses. Western wheatgrass, blue grama, green needlegrass, buffalo grass, and Junegrass are a few grasses found on North America's mixed prairies.

Steppes are also grasslands. Eastern Europe and Asia have vast steppes. Steppes are often hot and dry, with short grasses. America's short-grass prairies, just east of the Rocky Mountains, are also dry.

Savannas are yet another type of grassland. Coarse grasses grow on the savanna in large patches, with trees and shrubs dotting the landscape.

Each type of grassland supports different kinds of life. Large herds of buffalo once roamed North America's prairies. Elephants, on the other hand, are native to Africa and Asia.

OTHER GRASSLAND PLANTS

Grass isn't the only grassland plant. Small trees may grow in different areas. Herbs and wildflowers, sometimes called **forbs**, make meadows beautiful.

Shooting stars thrive in prairies and meadows. They're also called prairie pointers, birdbills, or American cowslips. Other flowering plants found in North America's prairies include heath aster, annual sunflower, lazy daisy, primrose, Indian paintbrush, and butterfly weed. Goldenrod, daisies, and peonies also thrive in grassy areas.

Walk through a grassy area near you. Enjoy the different plants thriving there.

WHAT'S THAT BUZZ?

Grasses, wildflowers, and other meadow plants are a magnet for insects. Indeed, with over 750,000 different species, insects thrive in habitats throughout the world.

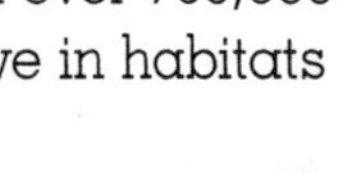

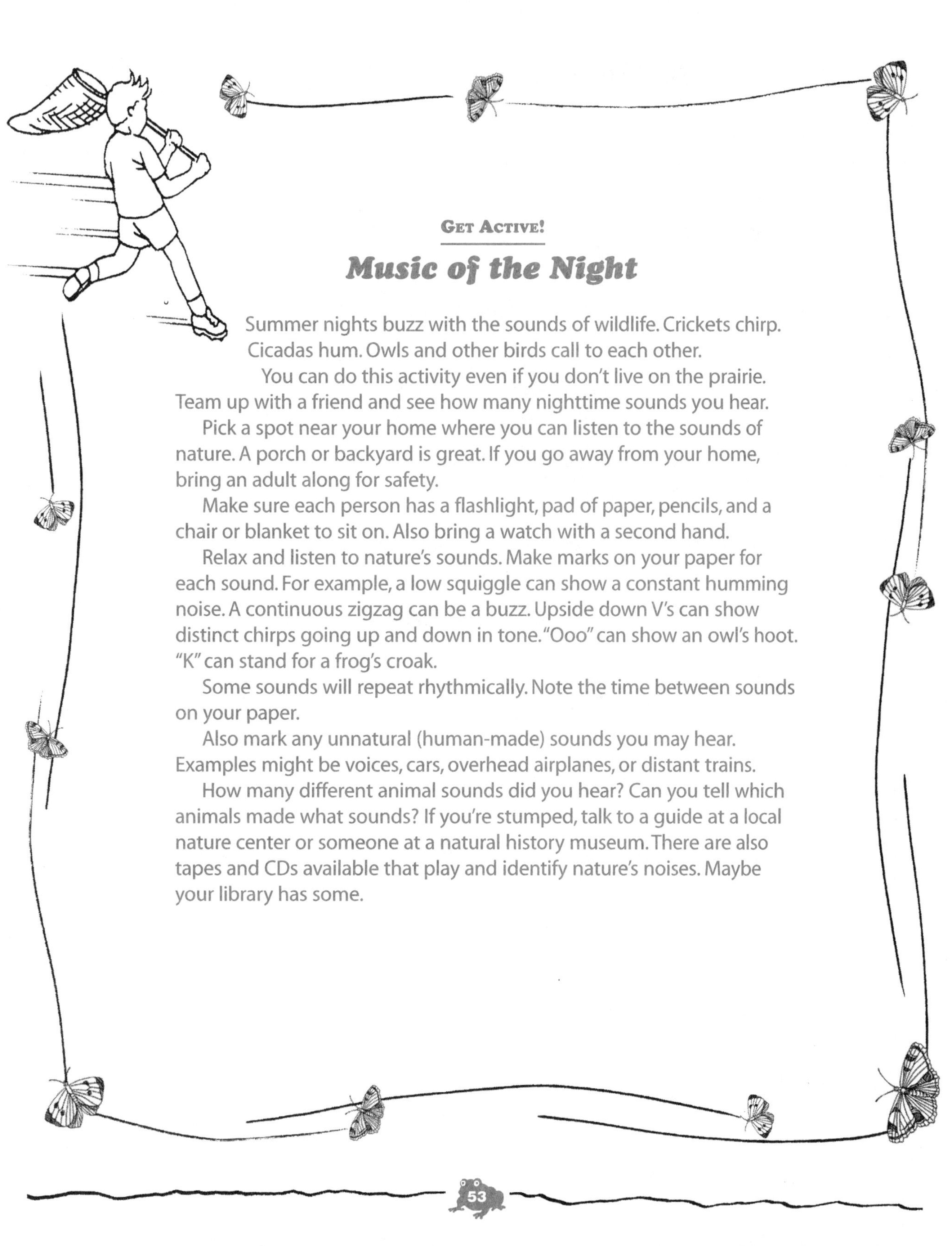

GET ACTIVE!

Music of the Night

Summer nights buzz with the sounds of wildlife. Crickets chirp. Cicadas hum. Owls and other birds call to each other.

You can do this activity even if you don't live on the prairie. Team up with a friend and see how many nighttime sounds you hear.

Pick a spot near your home where you can listen to the sounds of nature. A porch or backyard is great. If you go away from your home, bring an adult along for safety.

Make sure each person has a flashlight, pad of paper, pencils, and a chair or blanket to sit on. Also bring a watch with a second hand.

Relax and listen to nature's sounds. Make marks on your paper for each sound. For example, a low squiggle can show a constant humming noise. A continuous zigzag can be a buzz. Upside down V's can show distinct chirps going up and down in tone. "Ooo" can show an owl's hoot. "K" can stand for a frog's croak.

Some sounds will repeat rhythmically. Note the time between sounds on your paper.

Also mark any unnatural (human-made) sounds you may hear. Examples might be voices, cars, overhead airplanes, or distant trains.

How many different animal sounds did you hear? Can you tell which animals made what sounds? If you're stumped, talk to a guide at a local nature center or someone at a natural history museum. There are also tapes and CDs available that play and identify nature's noises. Maybe your library has some.

Black-Footed Ferrets

Sometimes people's actions have unintended consequences. Just look at the black-footed ferret.

Farmers' efforts to get rid of prairie dogs almost wiped out the black-footed ferret. Black-footed ferrets are small, weasel-like mammals. They eat prairie dogs.

When farmers began killing prairie dogs, many ferrets died from eating poisoned animals. Other methods of killing prairie dogs reduced the natural food supply for this ferret species. At one point, almost none remained.

To keep black-footed ferrets from becoming extinct, scientists rounded up 18 black-footed ferrets. They began breeding them in captivity.

In 1994, scientists released ferrets back into Badlands National Park. The federal park in South Dakota has a large prairie dog population, so the ferrets have lots to eat. The black-footed ferret survived, but the species had a close call.

Buffalo

Tens of millions of buffalo once roamed North America's prairies. Buffalo were a major food source for native tribes.

As settlers moved westward during the nineteenth century, they declared war on the buffalo. Some people killed these animals for their fur. Others killed them for their tongues. Many were shot either "for fun" or because farmers deemed them a nuisance. Rotting buffalo bodies became a common sight. By the beginning of the twentieth century, there were almost no buffalo running free on the American prairies.

Finally, people set aside lands to try to save the buffalo. Some areas also began raising buffalo, much the same way farmers raise cattle. Buffalo could not only be saved, but even used again for food.

In 1993, the Nature Conservancy released 300 buffalo onto Oklahoma's Tallgrass Prairie Preserve. The preserve has more than 500 species of native plants to feed the wild buffalo. While buffalo are still raised for agricultural purposes, it's good to know that some buffalo can once again run free in nature.

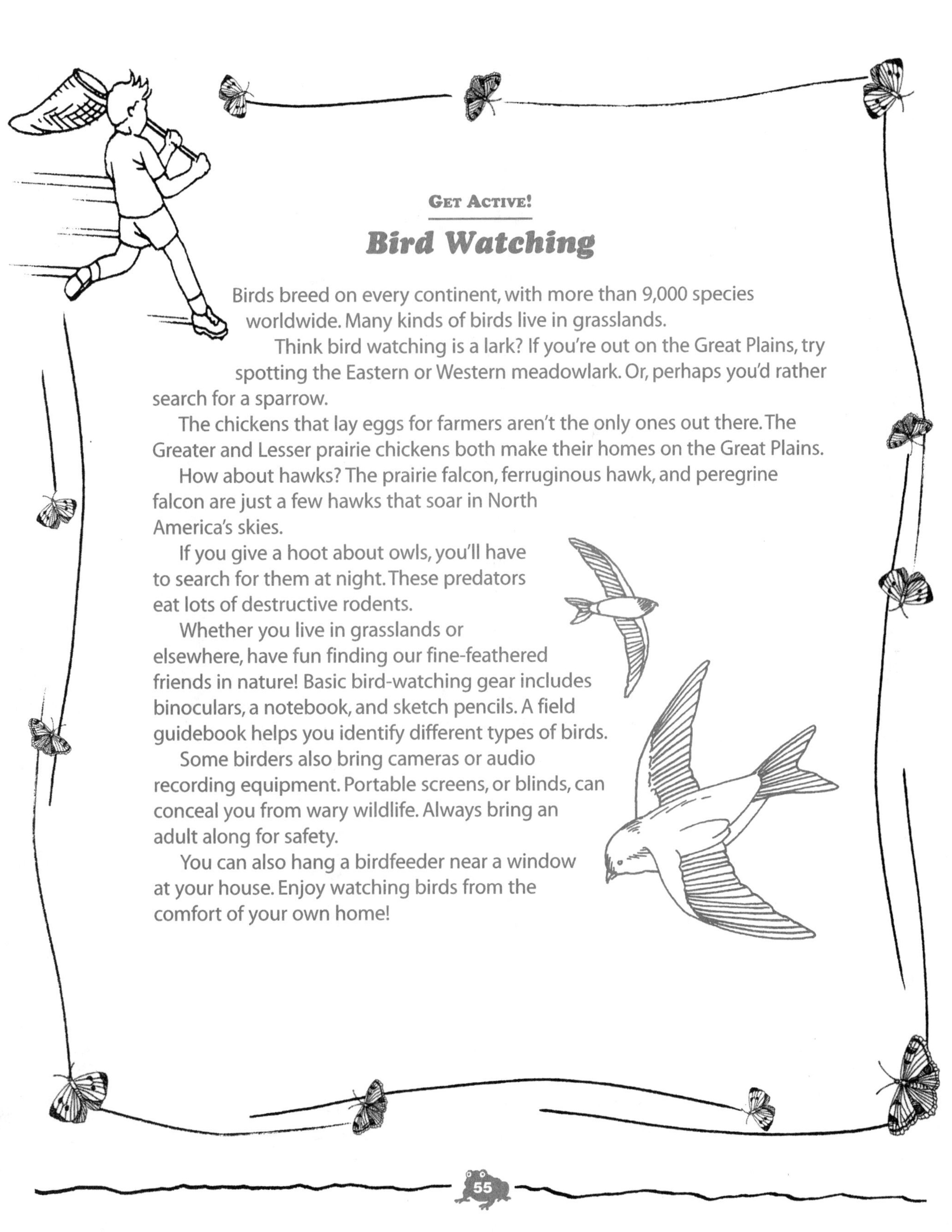

GET ACTIVE!

Bird Watching

Birds breed on every continent, with more than 9,000 species worldwide. Many kinds of birds live in grasslands.

Think bird watching is a lark? If you're out on the Great Plains, try spotting the Eastern or Western meadowlark. Or, perhaps you'd rather search for a sparrow.

The chickens that lay eggs for farmers aren't the only ones out there. The Greater and Lesser prairie chickens both make their homes on the Great Plains.

How about hawks? The prairie falcon, ferruginous hawk, and peregrine falcon are just a few hawks that soar in North America's skies.

If you give a hoot about owls, you'll have to search for them at night. These predators eat lots of destructive rodents.

Whether you live in grasslands or elsewhere, have fun finding our fine-feathered friends in nature! Basic bird-watching gear includes binoculars, a notebook, and sketch pencils. A field guidebook helps you identify different types of birds.

Some birders also bring cameras or audio recording equipment. Portable screens, or blinds, can conceal you from wary wildlife. Always bring an adult along for safety.

You can also hang a birdfeeder near a window at your house. Enjoy watching birds from the comfort of your own home!

Featured Creature

Giraffes

Giraffes easily measure up as the world's tallest animal. Some of these African savanna dwellers are more than 19 feet (5.8 m) tall. That's as tall as three grown men!

Giraffes' long necks let them reach leaves on acacia trees. The giraffe's 18-inch (46 cm) tongue strips the leaves right off the branches.

Giraffes bend down low too. They like eating the tall grass on the savanna. Interestingly, giraffe necks have the same number of bones as your neck—seven.

Giraffes' long-legged gait looks funny. Both front legs move forward, and then both back legs move. As the giraffe's head bobs up and down, it looks almost like a rocking horse. But when danger nears, giraffes run very quickly.

If a giraffe gets cornered, it uses its legs another way. Its powerful kick can sometimes kill a lion. Lions are giraffes' main predator.

Giraffe spots stand out at the zoo. In their African home, however, the spots are a type of camouflage. When giraffes stand under a tree, the spots look like leaf shadows.

Surprisingly, no two giraffes have exactly the same pattern of spots. Just as fingerprints help identify people, spots help identify individual giraffes. By learning about their spots, scientists can better track giraffes in the wild.

Insect bodies have three parts: a head, **thorax** (middle part), and abdomen. Insects' six legs connect to the thorax.

Many insects fly, including bees, mosquitoes, wasps, flies, beetles, moths, and butterflies. Their wings attach to the thorax.

Some insects seem to be just plain pests. Mosquitoes, wasps, and flies bite. Locusts and other insects eat farmers' crops.

But some insects are very helpful. Some, like the praying mantis, feed on insects that otherwise would harm crops.

Others, like bees, help **pollinate** plants. Bees pick up pollen on their feet as they suck nectar from flowers. As they fly from flower to flower, they spread the pollen. That helps plants make seeds. Bees then carry nectar back to their hives where they make honey from the nectar. The honey you spread on biscuits and toast is made by bees.

Bees have an interesting social life. The queen bee in the hive lays up to 1,500 eggs daily. Male bees, called drones, fertilize the eggs. The great majority of bees are worker bees. They cannot breed. Instead, they gather nectar and make honey to feed the whole hive. When you hear the phrase, "busy as a bee," think about these buzzing workers.

WORDS to KNOW

thorax: middle part of an animal's body (as on an insect); chest. [THOR-ax]

pollinate: spread flower pollen in a way that helps the plant reproduce. [POL-in-ate]

THE AFRICAN SAVANNA

Africa's tropical savanna is much warmer than the American prairie. Broad areas of coarse grass grow here, along with low shrubs and small, scattered trees.

Giraffes, wildebeests, zebras, ostriches, African elephants, and a host of other animals coexist here. They feed on different parts of the grasslands. After feasting on an area, the animals move on, seeking fresh supplies of food.

The savanna has predators too. Lions and hyenas are especially dangerous to other animals.

NATURE STATS

A Really Big Bird

The ostrich is the world's biggest bird. It grows up to 9 feet (275 cm) tall. These native African birds cannot fly, but they can run up to 44 miles per hour (70 km/h). Now that's fast!

GET ACTIVE!

Zoo Safari

The next time you visit a zoo, note which animals come from the African savanna. See who in your group catches sight of the most savanna animals.

Also check out the type of enclosure the animals have. Forty years ago, small cages with bars were common in zoos. In recent decades, American zoos have made enclosures more like the animals' natural habitats. Landscaping similar to where the animal lives in nature makes the animals more comfortable. And it helps us understand these creatures and their habitats better.

Zoos do more than simply display animals. Many zoos support captive breeding programs for species that are threatened or endangered. Zoos also encourage conservation and teach people to respect the environment.

Find out what educational programs your local zoo has for kids. These programs not only teach you about animals, but they're lots of fun.

CHAPTER 6
DESERTS

WORDS to KNOW

desert: a dry habitat that receives less than 10 inches (25 cm) of precipitation annually. [DEZ-ert]

DRY LANDS

Making up one-seventh of Earth's land, deserts cover vast areas in Africa, North America, South America, Asia, and Australia. Deserts get very little precipitation—often less than 10 inches (25 cm) per year. Deserts also have high evaporation rates from wind, heat, and other factors. Thus, deserts are dry, parched areas.

Some deserts are cold deserts. Their winter daytime temperatures often drop below freezing (32°F or 0°C). The Great Basin Desert is a cold desert. It stretches over 158,000 square miles (411,000 sq. km) over parts of Idaho, Nevada, Oregon, and Utah. Other cold deserts include Argentina's Patagonian desert and the Gobi Desert in Mongolia and China.

Hot deserts, in contrast, often have summer daytime temperatures over 100°F (38°C). Winter daytime temperatures seldom sink below freezing.

Even hot deserts get chilly at night. Without cloud cover to hold heat close to Earth's surface, temperatures can drop 50°F (28°C) or more in a single night. When the sun rises, temperatures climb again.

NATURE STATS

The Driest Desert

South America's Atacama Desert is the driest desert on Earth. It lies mostly in northern Chile, between the Andes Mountains and the Pacific Ocean. On average, the Atacama Desert gets less than half an inch (1.3 cm) of rain each year. Now that's dry!

The hot Sonoran, Chihuahuan, and Mojave Deserts cover large areas of the southwestern United States. Their combined area is 320,000 square miles (832,000 sq. km). Together, these three deserts spread over parts of Arizona, California, New Mexico, Nevada, and Texas. The Sonoran and Chihuahuan Deserts also extend into Mexico.

Earth's largest hot desert is the Sahara. It stretches over 3.5 million square miles (9.1 million sq. km) in northern Africa. The Arabian Peninsula is covered by 1 million

Get Active!

Sculpt with Wind and Water

You need:
play sand
shallow baking pan
straw
water

CAUTION: Do this activity outside to make cleanup easier. Never blow sand into anyone's face.

1. Scoop play sand into the baking pan. Using the straw, blow air at the sand. See what shapes you can form.

   Wind on the desert sculpts sand into dunes and other land forms. Wind also speeds evaporation, which makes the desert drier than it might otherwise be.
2. Lift the pan slightly at one end. Gently pour water down and through the sand. What does the water do to the sand?

   What little rain deserts get sometimes falls as thunderstorms. Runoff easily erodes, or washes away, desert soil. The results are canyons and other land forms.

Some Desert Landforms	
Arroyo	Flat, dry streambed with steep sides.
Canyon	Steep, sculpted valley carved by a river in a high, rocky area. Arizona's Grand Canyon is 277 miles (446 km) long.
Dune	Molded sand mound built by blowing winds.
Playa	Flat surface with criss-crossing cracks caused by stormwater runoff.
Mesa	Flat "table top" of rock rising where water and wind washed away softer surrounding rock.
Butte	Landform with rounded or flat top and sloping sides. (Like a mesa, but smaller.)

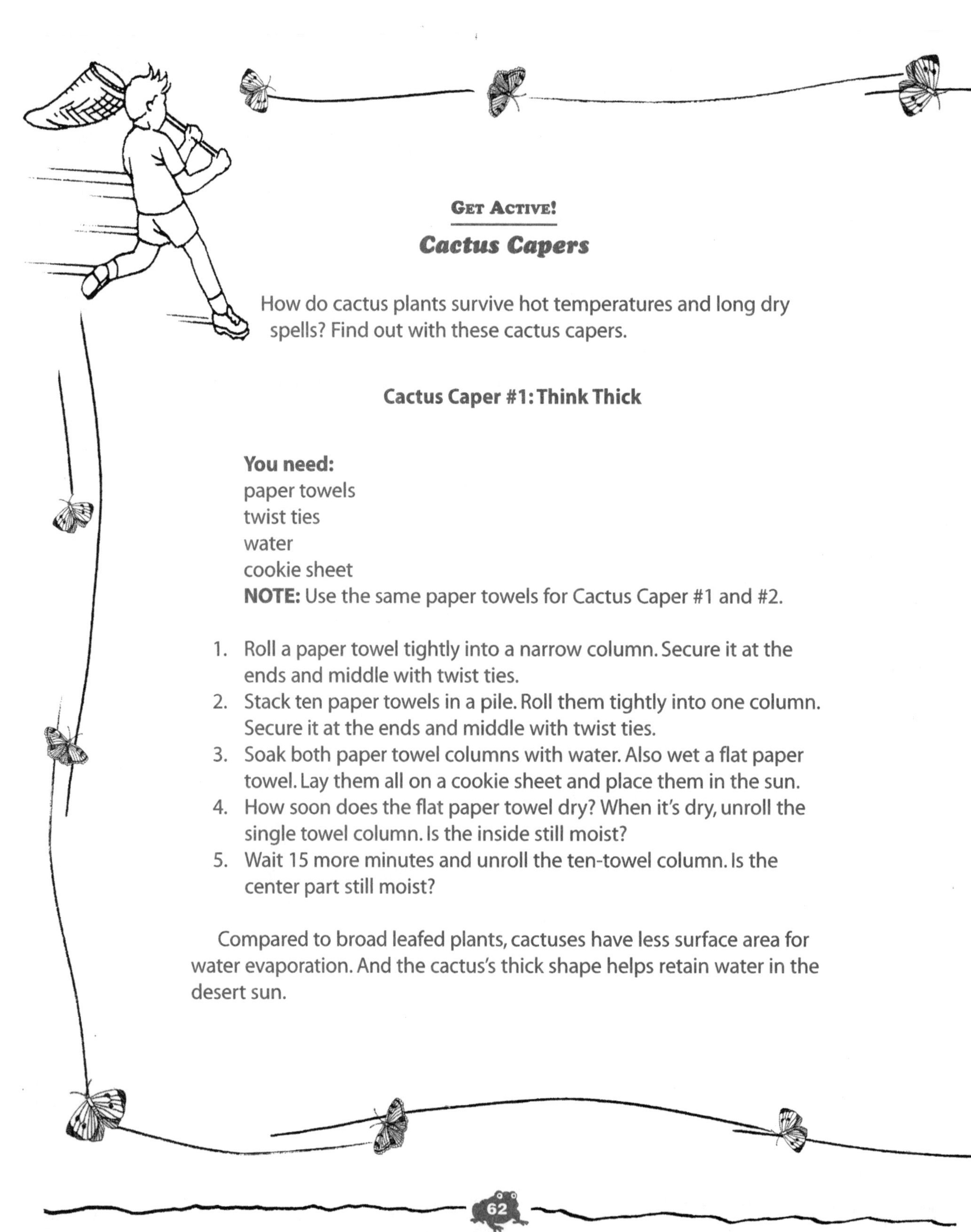

GET ACTIVE!

Cactus Capers

How do cactus plants survive hot temperatures and long dry spells? Find out with these cactus capers.

Cactus Caper #1: Think Thick

You need:
paper towels
twist ties
water
cookie sheet
NOTE: Use the same paper towels for Cactus Caper #1 and #2.

1. Roll a paper towel tightly into a narrow column. Secure it at the ends and middle with twist ties.
2. Stack ten paper towels in a pile. Roll them tightly into one column. Secure it at the ends and middle with twist ties.
3. Soak both paper towel columns with water. Also wet a flat paper towel. Lay them all on a cookie sheet and place them in the sun.
4. How soon does the flat paper towel dry? When it's dry, unroll the single towel column. Is the inside still moist?
5. Wait 15 more minutes and unroll the ten-towel column. Is the center part still moist?

Compared to broad leafed plants, cactuses have less surface area for water evaporation. And the cactus's thick shape helps retain water in the desert sun.

Get Active!

Cactus Capers

Cactus Caper #2: Why a Waxy Coating?

You need:
paper towels
twist ties
water
cookie sheet
waxed paper

1. Make two stacks of six paper towels. Roll each stack tightly into a column. Secure each column at the ends and in the middle with twist ties.
2. Soak both paper towel columns with water. Roll waxed paper around one column and secure it with more twist ties. Put both paper towel columns on the cookie sheet.
3. Place the cookie sheet in a warm, sunny spot. Wait 90 minutes then unroll them. Which paper towel column is wetter?

Cactuses' waxy covering works like the waxed paper on your paper towels. It keeps moisture in.

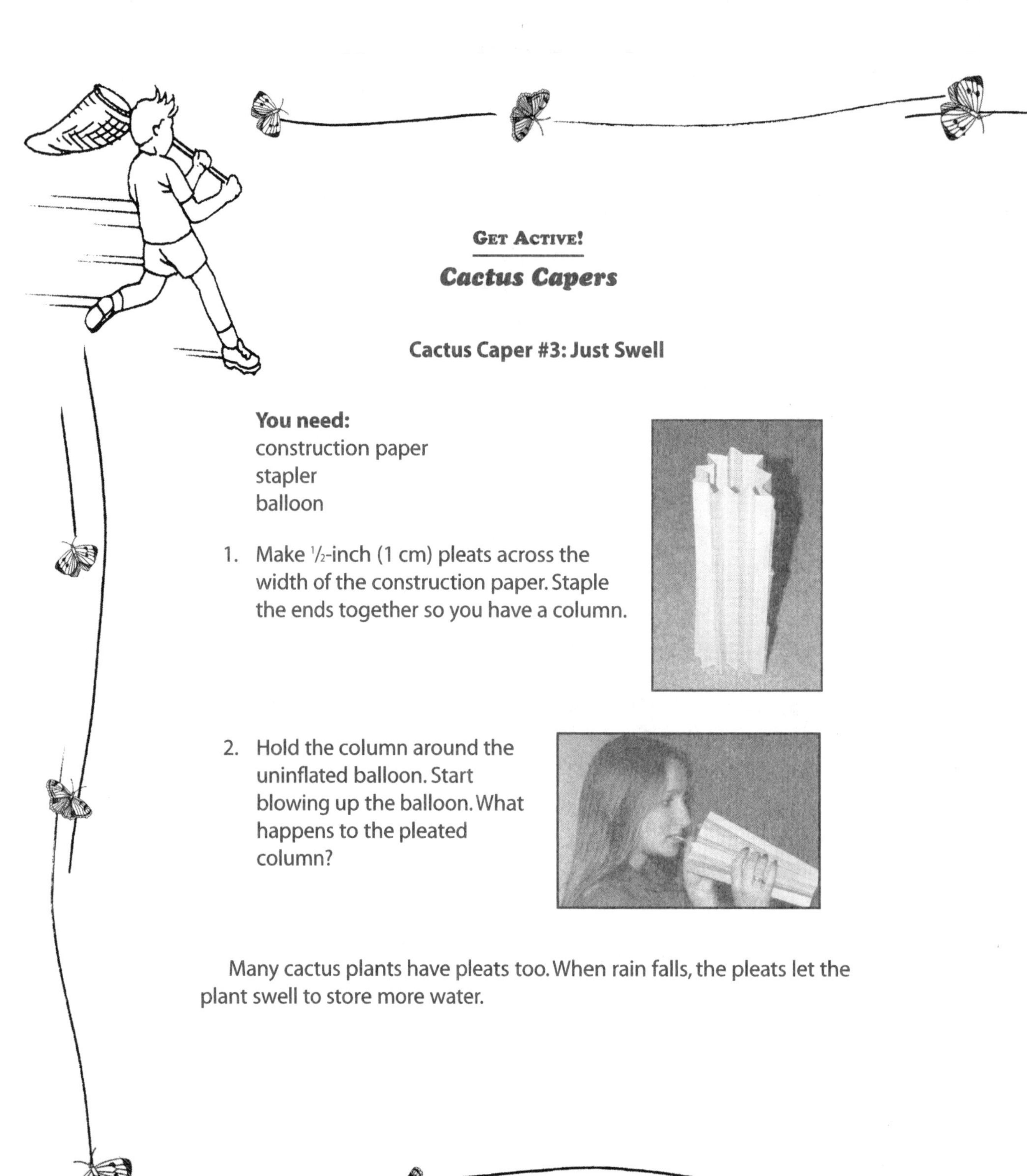

GET ACTIVE!

Cactus Capers

Cactus Caper #3: Just Swell

You need:
construction paper
stapler
balloon

1. Make ½-inch (1 cm) pleats across the width of the construction paper. Staple the ends together so you have a column.

2. Hold the column around the uninflated balloon. Start blowing up the balloon. What happens to the pleated column?

Many cactus plants have pleats too. When rain falls, the pleats let the plant swell to store more water.

GET ACTIVE!

Cactus Capers

Cactus Caper #4: Making a Point

You need:
rectangular block of floral foam
pins
flashlight

1. Stick about 20 pins onto one long side of the block so they look like cactus needles. Leave the other sides alone.
2. Dim the room lights. Hold the flashlight about two feet (61 cm) away. Shine it at a 45-degree angle to different sides of the block. Notice how the pins cast shadows.

Cactus needles cast small shadows too. Those shadows help protect the cactus from scorching sunshine. They also block some winds that would speed water evaporation.

Cactus needles have sharp barbs that keep most animals away. Otherwise, the animals would break open the cactus to get at its juicy inside.

So, what's the point of cactus needles? The point is to protect the cactus!

square miles (2.6 million sq. km) of desert. About the same area of hot desert blankets one-third of Australia.

Deserts are dry, but they are not deserted. An amazing array of plants and animals survive in the desert.

It's a Natural Fact!

Desertification

Grasslands can sometimes change to deserts if there is a long drought. Overgrazing or too intense farming can speed the process.

Desertification can be a serious problem. During the 1980s and 1990s, parts of Africa's Sahel region grew very arid. Crops failed, and many people died in the resulting famine.

TYPES OF CACTUS

There are more than 1,600 species of cactus! These cactuses all grow in the southwestern United States:

Saguaro Cactus	As North America's largest cactuses, Saguaros can grow to over 36 feet (10 m) tall. But they grow slowly. A 25-year-old Saguaro may be just 2 feet tall! Some Saguaros in the Sonoran desert are hundreds of years old.
Prickly Pear Cactus	These cactuses look like groups of needle-covered paddles. The flat shape minimizes the area exposed to sun overhead. The plant's egg-sized fruits are used in prickly pear jelly.
Barrel Cactus	These cactuses' squat, round shapes and pleated design make them look like barrels.
Pincushion Cactus	Growing close to the ground, these cactuses look like clusters of pincushions with needles stuck in them.
Old Man Cactus	Instead of needles, white hairy structures cover this cactus.
Feather Cactus	Feathery clusters of spines cover this cactus.
Strawberry Cactus	This cactus' fruit looks like a strawberry with spines.
Cereus	This cactus' columns can grow 20 feet (6 m) high. It blooms only at night.
Hedgehog Cactus	Bright fuchsia flowers bloom each spring on this Sonoran desert cactus.
Organ-Pipe Cactus	Clusters of narrow cactus stems branch up from ground level on this featured plant at Arizona's Organ Pipe National Monument.

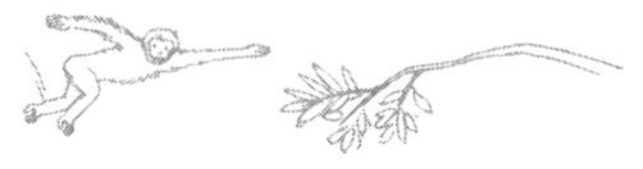

GETTING ALONG WITH CACTUS

The gila woodpecker is literally right at home with the Saguaro cactus. It bores a hole into it for a nest. To keep from drying out, the Saguaro forms a tough seal around the hole. In return for a home, the woodpecker eats insects that could harm the cactus.

The next year, the woodpecker moves on to a new nest. Elf owls, lizards, and even rabbits set up housekeeping in abandoned woodpecker holes.

White-winged doves often build nests on Saguaro arms. The cactus needles keep predators away from the bird.

keystone species: an organism upon which a significant number of other species depend for their survival in a particular habitat.

Woodrats like cactuses too. They build their nests near the plant's base. Cactus needles keep kit foxes and other predators out.

Because the Saguaro plays such an important role in the Sonoran Desert, scientists call it a **keystone species**. Without the Saguaro, many desert animals would be homeless!

GET ACTIVE!

Darker Is Cooler

You need:
2 buckets
sand
thermometer
waxed paper

1. Fill two buckets with sandbox sand. Early in the morning, put one bucket where the sun shines all day. Put the other bucket in a shaded spot. The temperature of the two spots should be about equal when you start.
2. Cover the thermometer with waxed paper to protect it from scratches. Measure the sand's temperature near the top of each bucket around noon. Repeat the procedure at 3:00 P.M. Which bucket's sand was warmer each time?
3. Measure the temperature in the sunny bucket again, but this time gently work the thermometer down about six inches (15 cm) into the bucket. Wait 10 minutes. Then check the temperature. Deeper is cooler in the desert too.

ephemeral: short-lived. [ee-FEM-er-ul]

CACTUSES AREN'T THE ONLY PLANTS

Golden poppies, pink clover, yellow brittlebush, and blue lupine dot large areas of the Sonoran Desert soon after spring rains. These plants are **ephemeral**, or short-lived.

Ephemeral plants sprout quickly after desert storms. When the weather dries up again, they wither and die. In between, they blossom brightly and produce seeds. The seeds have special coatings. They keep the seed from sprouting until the next heavy rains come.

Other plants deal with dry spells differently. The mesquite tree grows near gullies and dry riverbeds. Its long tap roots draw water from deep underground. In contrast, other plants have shallow roots that spread over a large area.

Yuccas use some of the same survival strategies as cactuses. The Joshua tree, for example, has hairy spines covering its trunk. The tree's leaves are long and narrow.

The ocotillo plant is also called the fire thorn or coachwhip plant. This southwestern American plant drops its leaves during parched periods, which helps it conserve moisture.

The creosote bush's poisonous roots keep other plants from crowding in. This lets the bush's roots spread out to soak up scarce water.

DEALING WITH DRYNESS AND HEAT

In a hot desert, scorching summer sun can make ground temperatures soar above 170°F (77°C). That's as hot as a roasted turkey!

Sidewinder snakes swish along in an S shape. As they move, only two parts of their long bodies touch the ground at any one time. This way, the snake minimizes contact

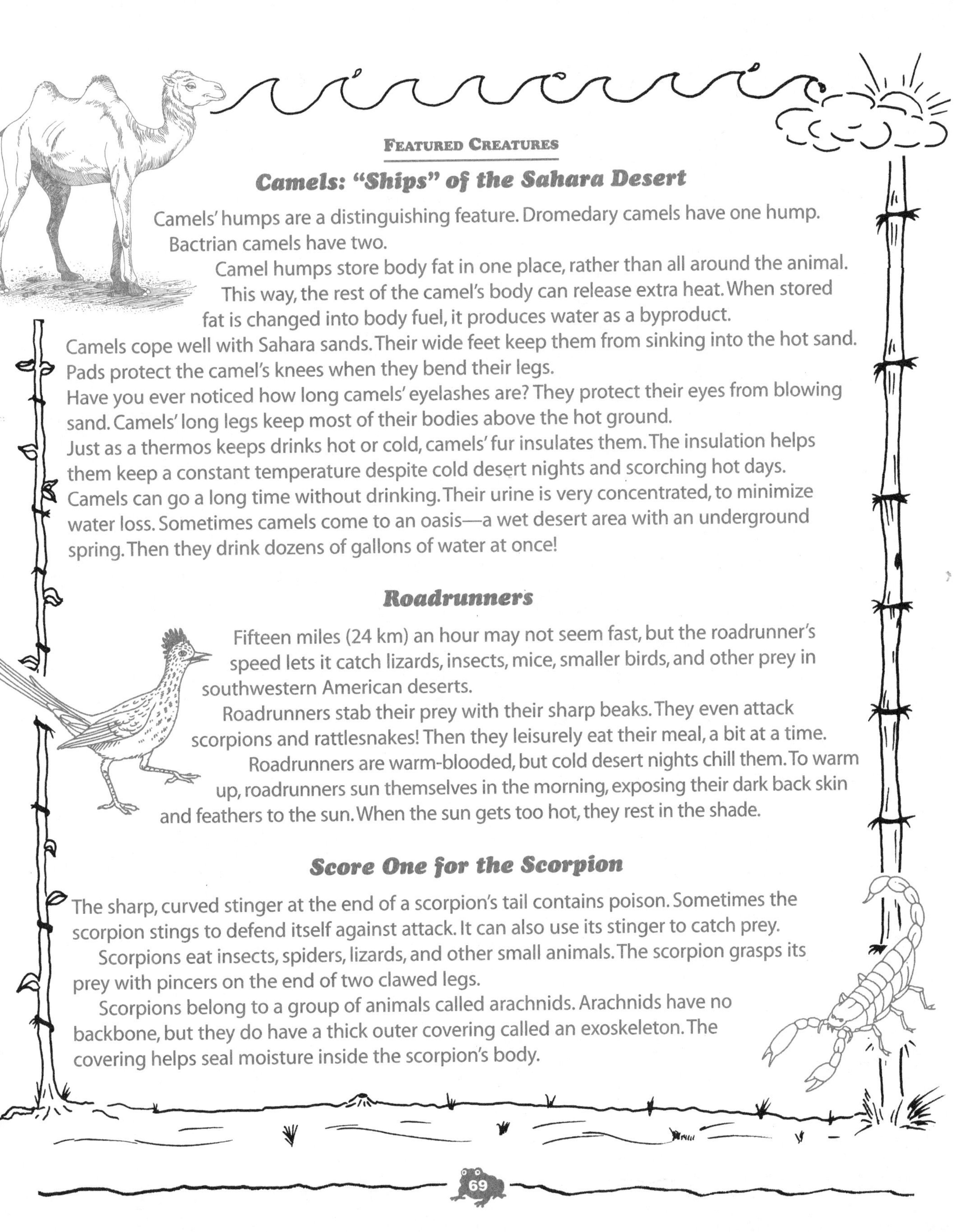

Camels: "Ships" of the Sahara Desert

Camels' humps are a distinguishing feature. Dromedary camels have one hump. Bactrian camels have two.

Camel humps store body fat in one place, rather than all around the animal. This way, the rest of the camel's body can release extra heat. When stored fat is changed into body fuel, it produces water as a byproduct.

Camels cope well with Sahara sands. Their wide feet keep them from sinking into the hot sand. Pads protect the camel's knees when they bend their legs.

Have you ever noticed how long camels' eyelashes are? They protect their eyes from blowing sand. Camels' long legs keep most of their bodies above the hot ground.

Just as a thermos keeps drinks hot or cold, camels' fur insulates them. The insulation helps them keep a constant temperature despite cold desert nights and scorching hot days.

Camels can go a long time without drinking. Their urine is very concentrated, to minimize water loss. Sometimes camels come to an oasis—a wet desert area with an underground spring. Then they drink dozens of gallons of water at once!

Roadrunners

Fifteen miles (24 km) an hour may not seem fast, but the roadrunner's speed lets it catch lizards, insects, mice, smaller birds, and other prey in southwestern American deserts.

Roadrunners stab their prey with their sharp beaks. They even attack scorpions and rattlesnakes! Then they leisurely eat their meal, a bit at a time.

Roadrunners are warm-blooded, but cold desert nights chill them. To warm up, roadrunners sun themselves in the morning, exposing their dark back skin and feathers to the sun. When the sun gets too hot, they rest in the shade.

Score One for the Scorpion

The sharp, curved stinger at the end of a scorpion's tail contains poison. Sometimes the scorpion stings to defend itself against attack. It can also use its stinger to catch prey.

Scorpions eat insects, spiders, lizards, and other small animals. The scorpion grasps its prey with pincers on the end of two clawed legs.

Scorpions belong to a group of animals called arachnids. Arachnids have no backbone, but they do have a thick outer covering called an exoskeleton. The covering helps seal moisture inside the scorpion's body.

with the hot sand. Sideways slithering also gives traction on slippery, sinking sands.

Big ears aren't just good for hearing. Fennec foxes, kit foxes, jerboas, and desert hares actually give off heat from their ears. They stay cooler this way.

Kangaroo rats don't need to "drink" at all. Their bodies make water as a byproduct of the seeds they munch. Their urine is so concentrated, it's nearly dry. Because kangaroo rats and other rodents don't sweat, they save even more water.

The elf owl, kit fox, scorpion, and pack rat rest during the day. When night falls, they become active. Without sunshine and cloud cover to retain heat, even hot deserts get cool at night.

Some animals, like the desert ground squirrel, are active only in early morning and late afternoon. During the hottest part of the day, they rest under rocks or burrow into the sand. Just one foot (30 cm) down, the sand can be 60°F (33°C) cooler than the surface!

Other animals, like the jackrabbit and roadrunner, rest in shade when the sun's heat is strongest. Darker areas tend to be cooler.

Some desert animals just bow out when the weather is hottest. Some desert toads and tortoises sleep deeply during the hot summer months. Their deep sleep is called **estivation**. Pocket mice, kangaroo rats, and some other warm-blooded animals go into a state called **torpor**, which is like hibernation.

WORDS to KNOW

estivation: extended state of inactivity during periods of extreme heat. [ess-tih-VAY-shun]

torpor: sluggish inactivity. [TORR-por]

marsupial: type of mammal that carries newborn young in a pouch. [mar-SOOP-ee-ul]

AUSTRALIAN ORIGINALS

How fast can you hop? Kangaroos' powerful legs let

them jump across Australia's deserts and grasslands at speeds over 12 miles per hour (20 km/h). The kangaroo keeps its stability by using its long tail as a counterbalance.

Kangaroos are a kind of mammal called **marsupials**. Their babies, called joeys, are born alive. But they can't yet survive on their own. Instead, the newborn crawls into the mother's pouch. There it nurses on her milk and continues to grow. The joey emerges 8 months later, ready to face the world.

Australia is isolated from other continents. As a result, its wildlife has developed in unusual ways.

Wallabies are members of the kangaroo family, although they don't use their broad tails for support. The yellow-footed rock wallaby is especially agile as it jumps around rocks and boulder piles.

Koalas are also marsupials. Living in Australia's dry forests, they feed mainly on eucalyptus branches. Koala babies often cling to their mothers' backs once they're big enough to survive outside the pouch.

Bandicoots are also marsupials. Brown bandicoots eat ant larvae, fungi, and even scorpions.

Dingoes are wild Australian dogs. They were brought to Australia by its first people, the Aborigines. Dingoes live in family groups and eat mostly sheep and rabbits.

Perhaps the strangest Australian animal is the duck-billed platypus. Living near lakes and rivers, it seems to be part bird and part mammal. It has a ducklike face and webbed feet, and its young hatch from eggs. But the duck-billed platypus also has fur and mammary glands to nurse its young. Thus, scientists say it is a mammal.

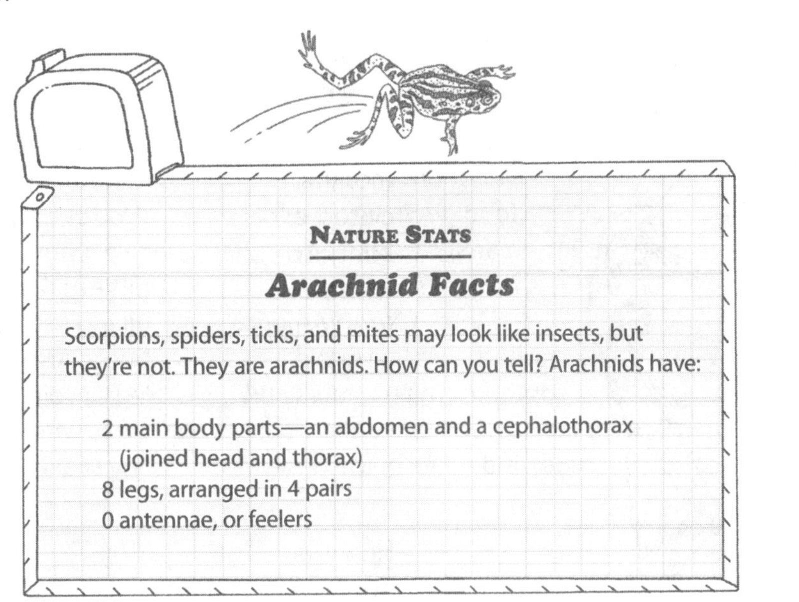

NATURE STATS

Arachnid Facts

Scorpions, spiders, ticks, and mites may look like insects, but they're not. They are arachnids. How can you tell? Arachnids have:

2 main body parts—an abdomen and a cephalothorax (joined head and thorax)
8 legs, arranged in 4 pairs
0 antennae, or feelers

Featured Creature

Don't Rattle a Rattlesnake

The rattlesnake's rattle is a warning. Watch out, it tells potential enemies, or I may attack. The rattle is made of bony parts at the end of the rattlesnake's tail.

Rattlesnakes don't always shake their rattles before attacking. When the rattlesnake hunts for food, it doesn't want to warn its prey.

Rattlesnakes eat mice, rats, gophers, birds, lizards, and frogs. Some rattlesnakes coil up tightly in a sheltered area. Other rattlesnakes blend into the surrounding soil and shadows. When prey comes near, they strike. As the rattlesnake bites, sharp fangs inject poisonous venom into the prey.

Rattlesnakes can't chew their food. Instead, they swallow it whole. Swallowing a meal can take hours. Then the rattlesnake's shape has a large bulge.

Digestion (breaking food down into useful parts) can take days or weeks.

Most of North America's rattlesnakes live in the southern United States and Mexico. Some, like the sidewinder, live in the desert. Others, like the eastern diamondback, prefer moist climates.

Rattlesnakes belong to a larger group called pit vipers. Pits on the snake's face detect heat from warm-blooded animals. Even in darkness, the pit sensors zero in on prey.

Rattlesnakes use their tongues for both taste and smell. Often they will flick their forked tongues into the air to smell for any prey.

Rattlesnakes' three layers of skin are formed into overlapping scales. Since they don't have eyelids, one layer of skin covers their eyes.

Although rattlesnakes grow throughout life, their outer skins don't. When rattlesnakes get too big, they shed their old skin.

Snakes play an important role in desert ecology. Among other things, they control rodents that can spread disease or destroy crops.

So, how can you avoid rattling a rattlesnake? Practice snake safety. If you're hiking in areas with rattlesnakes, wear thick boots. Also wear coverings on your lower legs. Avoid reaching into bushes or rocky areas where you can't see. And don't pick up any snakes you find in the wild.

CHAPTER 7
SURVIVING IN COLD CLIMATES

POLAR REGIONS: NORTH AND SOUTH

Earth's polar regions are more than cool. They're frigid! Winter temperatures drop as low as -70°F (-57°C). Summers rarely get warmer than 50°F (10°C).

lichen: fungus and algae that grow together as if they were one organism. [LYE-ken]

The Arctic tundra circles Earth's most northern lands. It includes parts of Scandinavia, Russia, Alaska, Canada, Iceland, and Greenland. To its north lies the Arctic Ocean, which is partly frozen all year round.

People often call Arctic areas the "land of the midnight sun." Because of Earth's tilt, these areas "point" toward or away from the sun, depending on the time of year. Thus, the Arctic summer is like one long day. Clyde River on Canada's Baffin Island has 24 hours of sunshine from May 13 to August 9.

In contrast, winter is really dark. The sun sets in Clyde River around November 22 and doesn't rise again until January 20. The most light it gets between then is a dim twilight between 9:00 A.M. and 2:00 P.M.

Also, because of Earth's tilt, Antarctica's seasons are reversed. While the Arctic region is shrouded in winter night, the Antartic is having nonstop summer sunshine.

Some types of natural life are found on both the Arctic tundra and in Antarctica. Both, for example, have **lichens** and insects. But some types are quite different. Polar bears prowl only on the Arctic tundra. Penguins only play in the chilly waters of the Southern Hemisphere.

Surviving bitter cold is a challenge for all life in the polar regions. Nature has ingenious ways for life forms to keep their cool, even in the bitter cold.

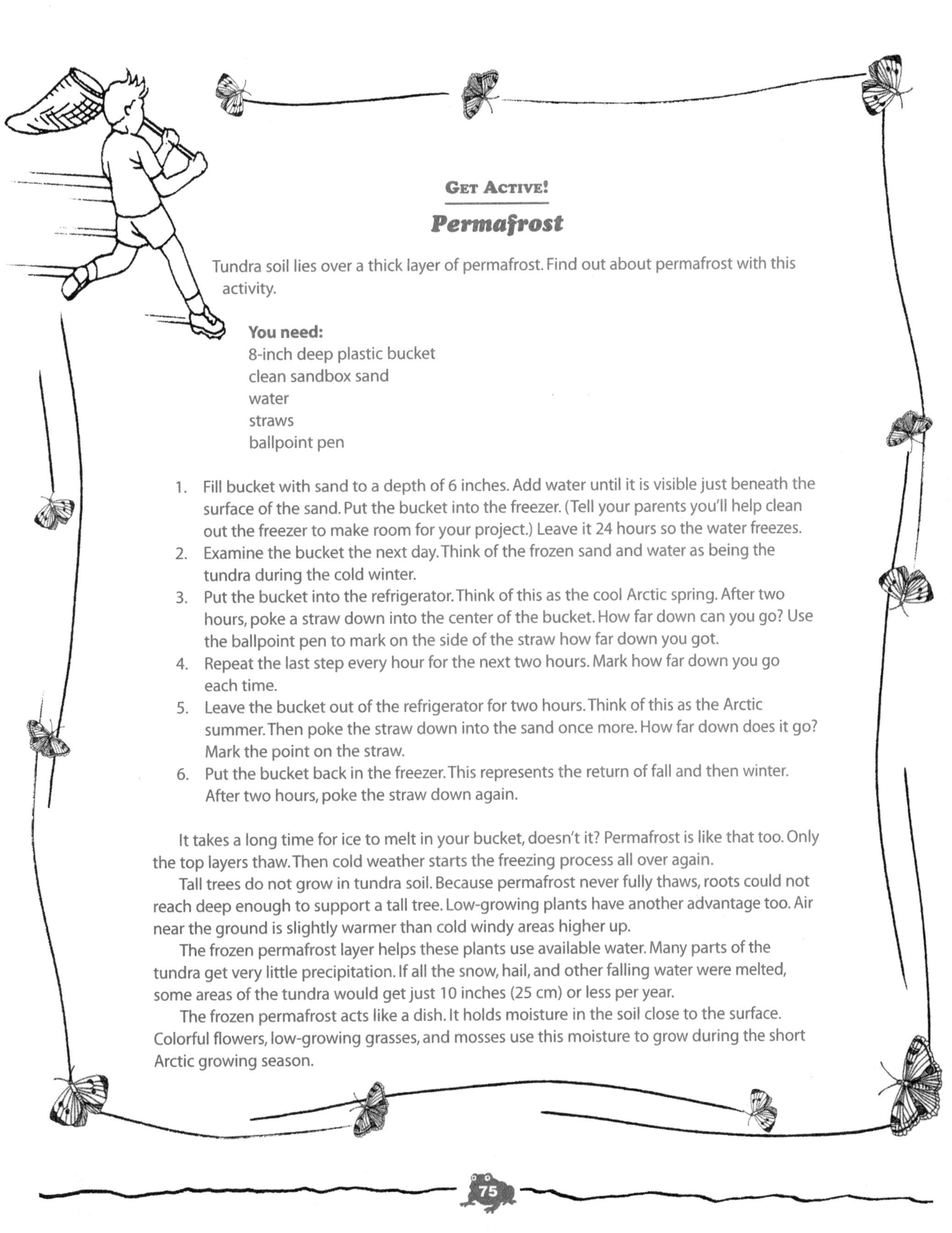

Get Active!

Permafrost

Tundra soil lies over a thick layer of permafrost. Find out about permafrost with this activity.

You need:
8-inch deep plastic bucket
clean sandbox sand
water
straws
ballpoint pen

1. Fill bucket with sand to a depth of 6 inches. Add water until it is visible just beneath the surface of the sand. Put the bucket into the freezer. (Tell your parents you'll help clean out the freezer to make room for your project.) Leave it 24 hours so the water freezes.
2. Examine the bucket the next day. Think of the frozen sand and water as being the tundra during the cold winter.
3. Put the bucket into the refrigerator. Think of this as the cool Arctic spring. After two hours, poke a straw down into the center of the bucket. How far down can you go? Use the ballpoint pen to mark on the side of the straw how far down you got.
4. Repeat the last step every hour for the next two hours. Mark how far down you go each time.
5. Leave the bucket out of the refrigerator for two hours. Think of this as the Arctic summer. Then poke the straw down into the sand once more. How far down does it go? Mark the point on the straw.
6. Put the bucket back in the freezer. This represents the return of fall and then winter. After two hours, poke the straw down again.

It takes a long time for ice to melt in your bucket, doesn't it? Permafrost is like that too. Only the top layers thaw. Then cold weather starts the freezing process all over again.

Tall trees do not grow in tundra soil. Because permafrost never fully thaws, roots could not reach deep enough to support a tall tree. Low-growing plants have another advantage too. Air near the ground is slightly warmer than cold windy areas higher up.

The frozen permafrost layer helps these plants use available water. Many parts of the tundra get very little precipitation. If all the snow, hail, and other falling water were melted, some areas of the tundra would get just 10 inches (25 cm) or less per year.

The frozen permafrost acts like a dish. It holds moisture in the soil close to the surface. Colorful flowers, low-growing grasses, and mosses use this moisture to grow during the short Arctic growing season.

LICHENS LIKE TUNDRA

Over 2,500 types of lichens grow in the Arctic tundra. Some tundra lichens look like peeling orange, yellow, or green paint. Others look like fuzzy pot scrubbers.

Lichens are not plants. They are really two other life forms growing together—a fungus and algae. The fungus gives the lichen support. It anchors the lichen to rock or soil. The algae uses the sun's energy to make food for itself and the fungus.

Together the two organisms have a symbiotic relationship. This means that they help each other survive. Oddly enough, if you were to grow the fungus and algae separately in a lab, they usually won't look anything like the lichen in nature. Both the fungus and the algae give the lichen in nature its color and texture.

Lichens play a crucial role in the Arctic ecosystem. Lichens feed caribou and other animals. Lichens also react with minerals in rock to help form soil. Plants can then grow in the soil.

IT'S A NATURAL FACT!

Flyways Are for the Birds

When North American birds fly south for the winter, they tend to follow similar paths, or flyways. The paths track major geographic features, like the Mississippi River valley or Allegheny Mountains. Just as interstate highways make travel easier for people, birds may find these flyways easier to navigate.

SUMMER FLOWERS

The most northern parts of the Arctic tundra are bare and rocky. But other areas bloom with summer flowers. Purple saxifrage blossoms early after winter snows melt. White Arctic bell-heather flowers drape gracefully. Spikes of bright pink fireweed flower in clumps. Marsh marigolds and Arctic buttercups sparkle with their bright yellow flowers.

Some Arctic plants even have tiny fruits. Bearberry, crowberry, and mountain cranberry grow well in the tundra climate.

Tundra plants often have small dark leaves that soak up the sun's warmth. Growing like a dense blanket, they also help keep the plant warm.

NATURE STATS

Lichens Around the World

About 20,000 different species of lichens grow around the world. Some thrive in the extreme cold. Others grow on mountains, in deserts, and other habitats.

One lichen, called oakmoss, grows in Europe and northern Africa. Manufacturers use it as a fixative in perfumes, soaps, and after-shave lotions. A fixative keeps a fragrance from evaporating too quickly.

Arctic flowers' bell shapes shelter summer insects from the cold. In turn, the insects help pollinate the flowers.

With a short growing season, Arctic plants grow only a small amount each year. During winter, most Arctic plants lie dormant under the snow.

BUG CITY

Dragonflies, blackflies, midges, mosquitoes, beetles, butterflies, moths, and bumblebees all have a field day when summer comes to the tundra. Swarms of more than a million insects per square yard (0.8 sq. m) buzz among summer bogs and puddles above the **permafrost** layer.

Mosquitoes and other insects make a tasty meal for many birds that spend summers in the Arctic. But the bugs in turn may "grab a bite" to eat from a nearby fox or other animal.

WORDS to KNOW

permafrost: permanently frozen ground. [PER-muh-frost]

MIGRATION

Have you ever noticed how many ads encourage travel to sunny resorts in the wintertime? Polar animals don't have travel agents. But many species do winter in warmer climates.

Caribou are reindeer. They live throughout the Arctic tundra. Both male and female caribou have antlers.

When cold weather comes, caribou migrate south in huge herds of a thousand animals or more. Winter is still cold for the caribou, but it is nowhere near as frigid as the tundra's bleakest regions.

Falcons, geese, gulls, and other birds also migrate south for the winter. These animals return again the next spring and summer.

WORDS to KNOW

hibernation: process by which warm-blooded animals slow their body processes to conserve energy and survive winter cold. [hye-ber-NAY-shun]

predator: animal that hunts another for food. [PRED-ah-tor]

prey: animal that is hunted by another for food. [PRAY]

The frequent flyer award for all animals goes to the Arctic tern. The Arctic tern spends summers in the cool Arctic region. When September comes, this bird heads south—11,000 miles (18,000 km) south! In fact, the Arctic tern flies to the southern end of South America, not far from Antarctica. When weather starts getting colder down south, the Arctic tern turns north again.

WARM FUR COATS

Musk oxen stay on the Arctic tundra all year long. Their thick furry coats keep them warm, even in freezing weather. When summer comes, the fur coat is too warm. So, the musk oxen shed their woolly fur undercoat. Then the musk oxen's fur starts growing again, so it will be ready for the next cold winter.

Other tundra animals have thick, furry coats too. Arctic foxes and Arctic hares look brownish-gray in summer. The color acts as camouflage. It lets them blend in with the surrounding tundra landscape.

Come winter, both the Arctic fox and Arctic hare look white. The seasonal change in fur color now lets them blend in with ice and snow. Now they can hide from predators, or better stalk their prey.

A LONG WINTER'S SLEEP

Hibernation helps some animals in the polar regions and elsewhere in the world survive cold winters. Hibernation shuts down almost all of an animal's life processes. Body temperature drops dramatically. The heartbeat slows. The animal seems to be barely alive. The tundra ground squirrel hibernates all winter. Outside of the Arctic, animals like hedgehogs, woodchucks, and certain kinds of bats cope with the cold by hibernating.

Other animals, such as polar bears, don't officially hibernate. Their body temperature and heartbeat stay fairly high. Nonetheless, they hunker down in snowy dens for long

FEATURED CREATURE

Polar Bears

What color is a polar bear? Polar bears look like they're cream-colored or light yellow. But their individual hairs are actually transparent and hollow. The skin underneath their fur is black!

The hairs transport the sun's energy to the bear's skin underneath. The black skin absorbs the heat to warm the bear.

Polar bears are huge. Males range anywhere from 660 pounds (300 kg) to over 2,000 pounds (900 kg). Females weigh 25-50 percent less than males.

Up to 40 percent of the polar bear's total weight is fat. Fat provides energy when food is scarce. Fat also keeps polar bears warm. It acts like an extra blanket under their thick fur coats.

Polar bears spend lots of time in and near the Arctic Ocean. Their streamlined shape and webbed paws let them swim up to four miles per hour (6.5 km/h). That's the speed of an adult person's brisk walk.

Polar bears are fierce predators. A **predator** is an animal that hunts another animal, called the **prey**, for food. Polar bears' sharp, curved claws can break hard ice and grasp slippery prey in the ocean waters.

Sitting on top of the food chain, polar bears feed on seals and other animals. The seals, in turn, eat fish and shellfish that eat plankton.

But polar bears help other animals survive too. Given a choice, polar bears prefer the fatty parts of a seal. Those parts are easiest for it to digest. Arctic foxes, ravens, and gulls often feed on polar bears' leftovers.

Pregnant polar bears stay in snow dens from October until March or April. During the dark winter, they give birth to one to three cubs. Mothers rest inside the den, living off stored body fat. They nurse the cubs with fat-rich polar bear milk.

In the spring the cubs finally exit the den. Cubs often romp playfully with each other during the two and a half years they stay with their mother. As they grow, polar bear cubs learn to survive in the Arctic's cold climate.

periods during harsh winter weather. Animals outside the Arctic region who also bed down for a long winter rest include grizzly bears, raccoons, chipmunks, and skunks.

Only warm-blooded animals are true hibernators. Cold-blooded animals cannot regulate their own temperature. Rather, animals like insects, reptiles, and amphibians are the same temperature as their surroundings. Some, like the Monarch butterfly, migrate. Others, like turtles, toads, snakes, and earthworms, go into a deep sluggish state. They seem to be in suspended animation until spring brings warmth again.

tundra: a cold habitat found in northern polar regions or high mountains. [TUN-druh]

ALPINE TUNDRA

You probably live thousands of miles away from the polar regions. But you may be able to visit another naturally cold climate—alpine **tundra**. Alpine tundra is found in high mountain areas.

In the continental United States, Pike's Peak, Olympic National Park, Rocky Mountain National Park, and the White Mountain National Forest all have alpine tundra areas. Even in August, you'll feel chilly near the tops of these mountains. Other places in the world with alpine tundra include the Alps in Europe, the Himalayas in Asia, and Mount Kilamanjaro in Africa.

As on the Arctic tundra, plants and animals adapt to the alpine tundra's cold climate. Most plants are short and have brief growing seasons. A few alpine plants do sink deep roots into the soil. These roots not only anchor the plant, but prevent soil erosion on the mountain.

As in the Arctic, animals like weasels and ptarmigans change from brown to white as winter comes. The ptarmigan is a chicken-like ground bird that lives on both Arctic and alpine tundra.

Animals that migrate for winter don't have as far to travel. They just head down the mountains to lower areas. In the Tetons, for example, elk head down toward the National Elk

Refuge. Bighorn sheep in the Rocky Mountains move from high alpine ranges to lower, sheltered areas for the winter.

Some animals, like the marmot, hibernate. Marmots have furry brown backs and white bellies. The live in colonies of one male, two or three females, and their babies from the present and previous year.

Other small animals stay active throughout the winter on the alpine tundra. Rocky Mountain pikas look like small rabbits with little mouse ears. Pikas rarely grow bigger than 7 inches (18 cm) or weigh more than a pound (½ kg). In summer, they gather extra leaves, twigs, berries, and other plant matter. This is their winter food supply. Pikas stay active and warm during winter in dens sheltered by large rocks.

The alpine tundra's steep slopes present their own challenges. Different species of mountain goats are especially adapted to cliff life. They have powerful leg muscles and springy tendons. Their sturdy hooves have hard edges and spongy, gripping centers—somewhat like sneakers. These features help mountain goats leap from one ledge to another. Along the way, they munch on grass, moss, and lichens growing in sparse patches on the chilly alpine tundra.

GET ACTIVE!

Warming Up

Polar bears wouldn't stay as warm if their fur were white. See for yourself!

You need:

two identical mugs
water
rubber bands
two 6 x 6-inch (15 x 15 cm) white plastic squares (Cut from the top of a trash bag so the bottom part is still usable.)
two 6 x 6-inch (15 x 15 cm) pieces of clear plastic wrap
thermometer

1. Fill two mugs with water. Fasten two pieces of solid white plastic over one cup with a rubber band. Fasten two pieces of clear plastic over the other cup with another rubber band.
2. Put both mugs in a sunny spot. Wait two hours.
3. Remove the plastic from each cup. Measure the water temperature. Which mug's water is warmer?

White reflects up to 90 percent of the sun's energy, but clear plastic lets the sun's energy through. Likewise, transparent fur helps the polar bear stay warmer in its icy home.

Featured Creature

Penguins

Waddling on webbed feet, black and white penguins look like comical characters at a formal dinner. But why waddle? Sometimes it's easier for penguins just to toboggan along the ice on their bellies.

Penguins are most at home in the icy southern seas off Antarctica's coast. Penguins' bodies are specially made for swimming. Their webbed feet sit very close to their bodies. The feet work with the tail to help the penguin steer in the water.

Penguins cannot fly. Instead, their wings act like paddle flippers. They propel the penguin through chilly water.

Penguins preen their feathers often. Using their bills, penguins spread oil from near their tail on all the feathers. The feathers' overlapping pattern helps seal out wind and water. Downy tufts underneath trap air that keeps the penguins warm.

Swimming through the water, penguins hunt for food. Penguins eat lots of krill, which is a shrimplike crustacean. Different penguin species also eat squid and fish.

Penguins eat lots of food in the ocean. But they fast, or go without food, during mating and molting periods. (Molting is when feathers shed so new ones can grow in.)

The Emperor penguin is the largest penguin species. When it's time to breed, the male and female leave the water and go onto pack ice. Pack ice is a large block of ice that forms on the ocean surface.

After mating, the female Emperor penguin lays an egg. Hungry for food, she heads back to the ocean to hunt. Meanwhile, her mate keeps the egg warm. He keeps it off the ice by balancing it on his feathery feet. Then he drapes the egg with a flap of skin and feathers that hangs from his stomach.

Huddling together with hundreds of other males and their eggs, the father incubates the egg for two months in the dark, Antarctic winter. The huddling helps the father penguins warm themselves despite the bitter cold.

The mother returns in late winter as the young penguin hatches. She feeds the baby by regurgitating (throwing up) extra food she has eaten while away at sea. While she cares for the baby, the father heads off to eat. After all, he's very hungry after his months of guarding the egg!

CHAPTER 8
THE WATERY WORLD OF NATURE

WORDS to KNOW

specific gravity: measure of a material's density compared to distilled water.

hydrometer: instrument used to measure a liquid's specific gravity [hye-DROM-et-er]

WATER, WATER—ALMOST EVERYWHERE

Water covers about three-fourths of Earth's surface. From largest to smallest, the four oceans are the Pacific, Atlantic, Indian, and Arctic. Most seas connect to an ocean, such as the Mediterranean Sea or the Red Sea.

Which oceans and seas can you locate on a globe? About 50 percent of the United States' people live within an hour's drive of an ocean.

Sea water in oceans and seas makes up 97 percent of the world's water. Sea water is about 97 percent water, plus 3 percent dissolved chemicals. Sodium chloride—also called table salt—makes up 85 percent of the dissolved material. Another 12 percent is magnesium, sulfur, calcium, potassium, and carbon. Trace amounts of other chemicals are also dissolved. There's even a tiny bit of gold.

What's in a drop of sea water?

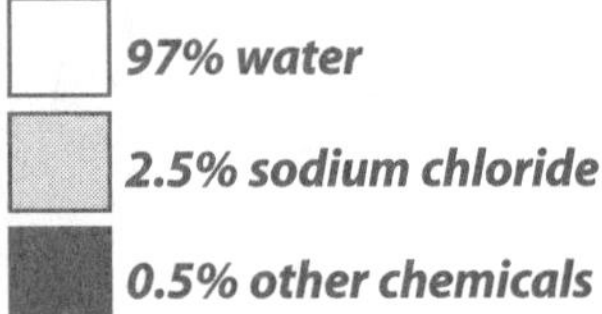

Two-thirds of the 3 percent of Earth's water that isn't sea water is ice. The remaining 1 percent of the world's water is fresh water. The Great Lakes are the largest fresh water lakes in North America. The Mississippi is North America's longest fresh water river.

Other watery environments are "in between" areas. Estuaries mix salt water with fresh water where rivers flow into oceans. Wetlands are land areas covered by water for all or part of the year.

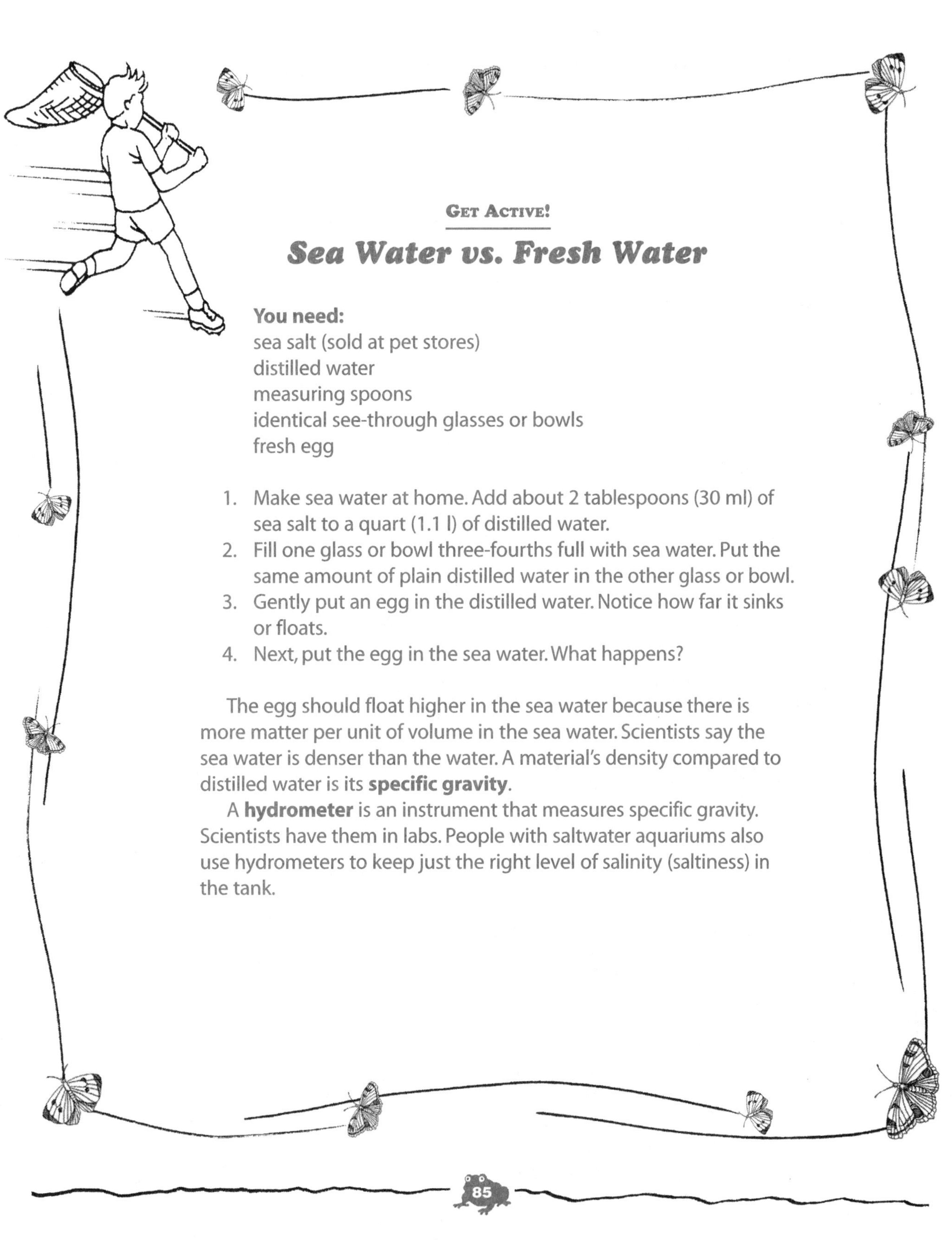

GET ACTIVE!

Sea Water vs. Fresh Water

You need:
sea salt (sold at pet stores)
distilled water
measuring spoons
identical see-through glasses or bowls
fresh egg

1. Make sea water at home. Add about 2 tablespoons (30 ml) of sea salt to a quart (1.1 l) of distilled water.
2. Fill one glass or bowl three-fourths full with sea water. Put the same amount of plain distilled water in the other glass or bowl.
3. Gently put an egg in the distilled water. Notice how far it sinks or floats.
4. Next, put the egg in the sea water. What happens?

The egg should float higher in the sea water because there is more matter per unit of volume in the sea water. Scientists say the sea water is denser than the water. A material's density compared to distilled water is its **specific gravity**.

A **hydrometer** is an instrument that measures specific gravity. Scientists have them in labs. People with saltwater aquariums also use hydrometers to keep just the right level of salinity (saltiness) in the tank.

WAVE WORDS

Crest	Highest point of a wave.
Trough	Lowest point of a wave.
Amplitude	Height of a wave from crest to trough.
Wavelength	Distance between waves, measured either from crest to crest or from trough to trough.
Swash	Wave water rushing up on the shore.
Backwash	Wave water rushing back to the sea.

SEAWEED BY THE SEASHORE

Giant kelp seaweed grows up to 200 feet long. Other seaweeds are smaller. All seaweeds use photosynthesis to make food from sunlight and carbon dioxide.

Next time you walk along a rocky beach, search for seaweed. You may find it washed up in a red, green, or brownish heap. If you spot seaweed growing in place, examine it, but don't move it.

Look for a holdfast. It anchors some seaweeds in place.

Next, try to spot bladders. These air pockets buoy seaweed up to the surface so it gets enough sunlight. Also search for stipes and blades. Stipes look like stems. Blades are leaflike structures.

Seaweeds play an important role in coastal ecology. They also provide useful things for people. Algae and seaweed products show up in items ranging from cream cheese and veggie burgers to toothpaste!

PLANKTON, FISH, AND MUCH, MUCH MORE

Phytoplankton forms the base of the ocean's food pyramid. These tiny bacteria and plants make their own food using photosynthesis.

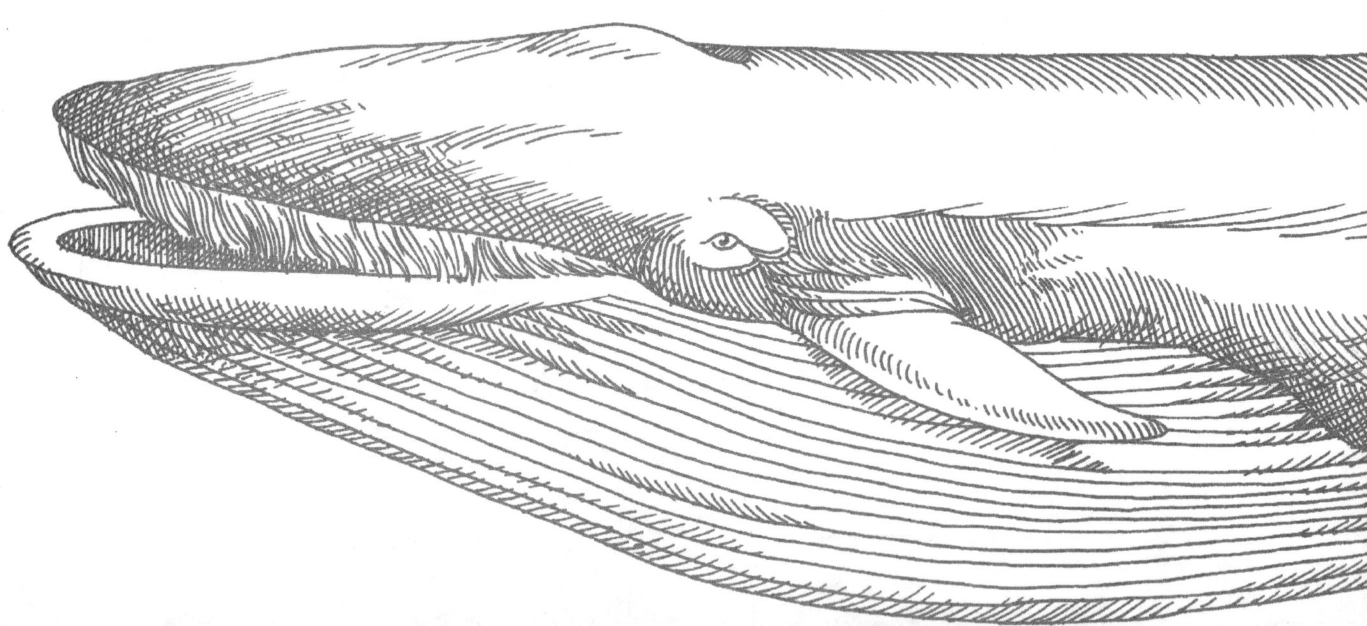

Zooplankton eat phytoplankton. Zooplankton include trillions of copepods. Copepods look like fleas and are about as big as rice grains.

In general, bigger marine life forms eat smaller organisms. Thus, in a simple food chain, a killer whale eats fishes that eat smaller sea creatures.

But the marine life food web can get complicated. The largest whales eat tiny creatures, such as krill. Some small organisms, like parasites or decomposers, attach themselves to and feed on larger life forms. Many animals eat various foods—not just one organism.

The greatest diversity of ocean life lives near the surface. Mollusks, like clams and scallops, have hard shells to protect them. Sea stars and other echinoderms have tough, spiny skins covering their soft bodies. Lobsters, crabs, and barnacles are examples of crustaceans.

Fish are the most obvious example of aquatic animals with backbones. Some live in oceans and seas. Others swim in fresh water lakes and streams.

Reptiles, such as sea turtles, also swim in the ocean. Many birds, including penguins, live by the sea too.

Even mammals make their homes in or near water. Whales and dolphins look like huge fish, but they are both mammals. They swim in the ocean, but surface to breathe air through their blowholes. Other marine mammals include seals, walruses, and manatees.

WORDS to KNOW

phytoplankton: tiny water-dwelling plants and bacteria that make their own food. [fye-toh-PLANK-tun]

zooplankton: tiny water-dwelling, single-celled organisms and animals that do not make their own food. [zoh-oh-PLANK-tun]

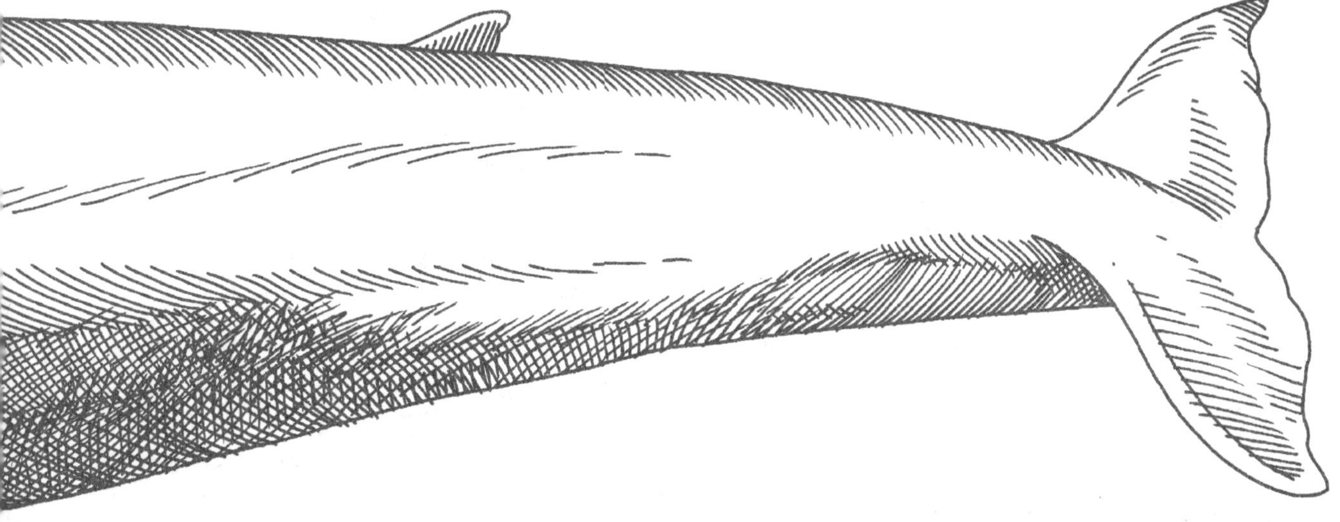

BEACHES AND TIDAL POOLS

Beaches are constantly being shaped by the ocean. Waves erode, or wear away, the beach in some spots. The waves deposit the sand further down.

Beaches are not just sandy shores. They're also rocky coastlines, cliffs, and other areas where the land meets the sea.

Coastlines are a beautiful part of nature. They're busy places too. Many plants and animals make their homes along the shore.

Tidal pools form where water collects on the coast. Daily tides affect their water levels. Tides are inward and outward flows of ocean water caused by the moon's gravity pull upon our rotating Earth.

Tidal pools form a special kind of water habitat. Anemones, sea stars, crabs, and many other animals thrive in tidal pools.

propulsion: forward movement, as by pushing. [proh-PUL-shun]

undulation: back-and-forth or sideways motion to propel oneself through water. [un-doo-LAY-shun]

hydrofoil: aerodynamic shape that creates pressure differences in a fluid. [HYE-droh-foyl]

liter: metric measure of volume, equal to approximately 1.056 liquid quarts. [LEE-ter]

GET ACTIVE!

Making Waves

You need:
½-**liter** plastic bottle
water
blue food coloring
1 cup peanut oil or vegetable oil

1. Fill a ½-liter clear plastic bottle half way with 1 cup (250 ml) water. Add 4 drops blue food coloring. Gently pour in 1 cup (250 ml) peanut or other clear vegetable oil. Cap the bottle tightly.
2. Watch the waves as you gently rock your "ocean in a bottle" back and forth.

Out on the ocean, blowing wind causes waves. Stormy weather can stir up giant waves. Underwater earthquakes and volcanoes can also set off gigantic waves, called tsunamis.

Most ocean waves move water in a circle: up, forward, down, and then flow back. At the shore, breaking waves rush up on the beach and then flow back. Waves striking the beach at an angle erode (wash away) parts of the beach. They deposit washed away sand and debris farther down the shore.

GET ACTIVE!

Ocean Motion

Some aquatic animals, like clams and coral, stay pretty much in one place. Others get around in different ways. Starfish and snails, for example, use tubular feet on their underside. Lobsters crawl along on their legs.

Put on your bathing suit, grab a balloon, and jump in a swimming pool. Experiment with ways marine animals move through the water.

CAUTION! Never swim by yourself or without adult supervision. Remove the balloon from the pool when you're done.

Jet propulsion

Blow up the balloon with air and hold the end closed. Then push the balloon underwater, aim, and let go. Jet propulsion pushes the balloon through the water.

Scallops, snails, octopuses, and some jellyfish also use jet **propulsion**. Instead of shooting out air, they squirt water to move along.

Rowing

Swim through the water with the breast stroke. Your arms act like oars to push you through the water. The butterfly fish and other fish with side fins also row through water.

Undulating

Put your feet together and arms by your side. Then wiggle your body like a snake. Wiggle forward and backward, and then sideways.

The wiggling is called **undulation**. The movements make waves. Sunfish, dolphins, and other animals use such waves to swim through the water.

Hydrofoil

Spread your arms and imagine you are an airplane. Then go underwater and push yourself through the water with your feet. Feel the water moving over your arms. Remember to come up for air!

Your arms are not **hydrofoils**, but penguin wings, seal flippers, and sea turtle flippers are. Like airplane wings, their shape creates differences in pressure underwater. The pressure differences help move these animals through water.

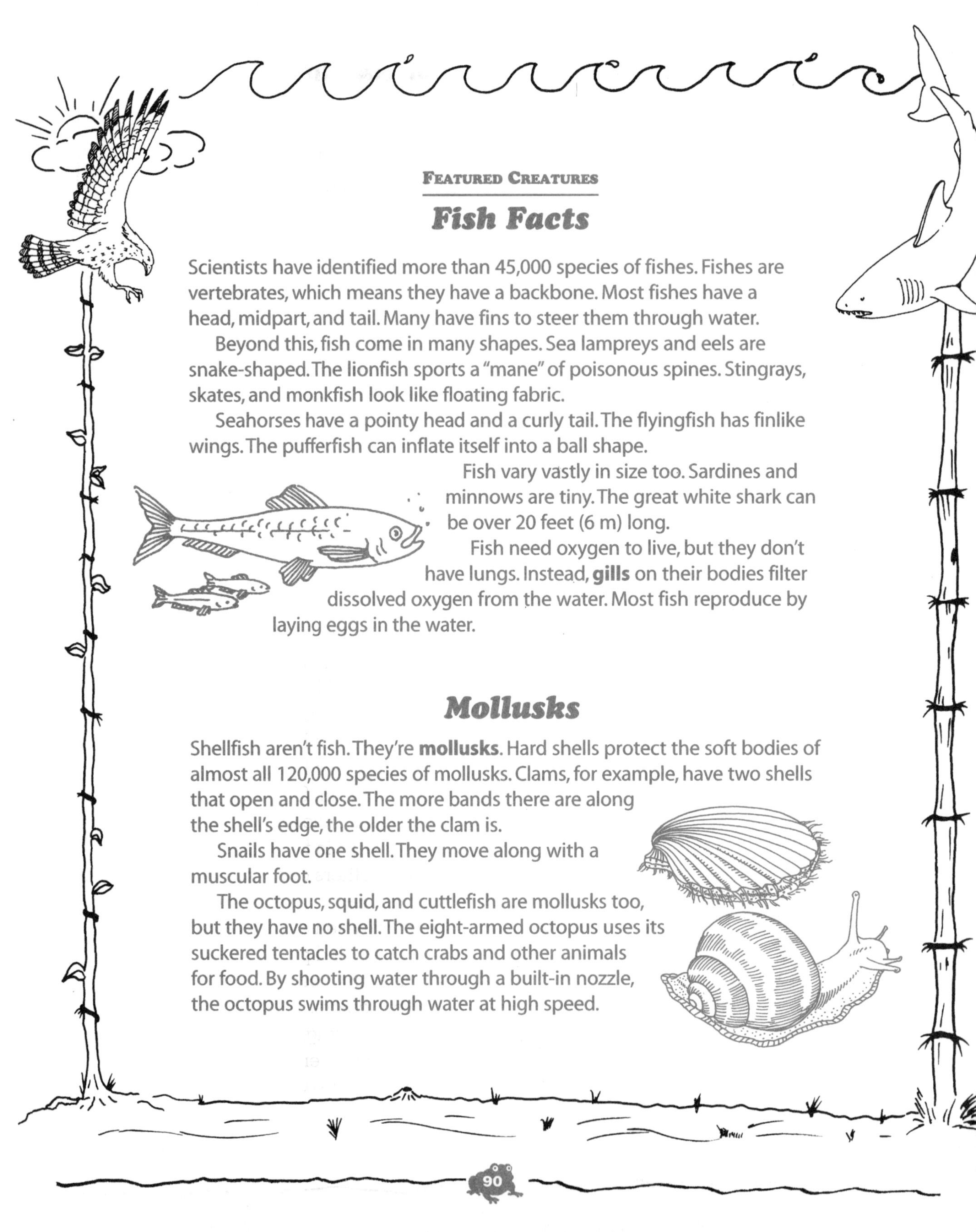

Fish Facts

Scientists have identified more than 45,000 species of fishes. Fishes are vertebrates, which means they have a backbone. Most fishes have a head, midpart, and tail. Many have fins to steer them through water.

Beyond this, fish come in many shapes. Sea lampreys and eels are snake-shaped. The lionfish sports a "mane" of poisonous spines. Stingrays, skates, and monkfish look like floating fabric.

Seahorses have a pointy head and a curly tail. The flyingfish has finlike wings. The pufferfish can inflate itself into a ball shape.

Fish vary vastly in size too. Sardines and minnows are tiny. The great white shark can be over 20 feet (6 m) long.

Fish need oxygen to live, but they don't have lungs. Instead, **gills** on their bodies filter dissolved oxygen from the water. Most fish reproduce by laying eggs in the water.

Mollusks

Shellfish aren't fish. They're **mollusks**. Hard shells protect the soft bodies of almost all 120,000 species of mollusks. Clams, for example, have two shells that open and close. The more bands there are along the shell's edge, the older the clam is.

Snails have one shell. They move along with a muscular foot.

The octopus, squid, and cuttlefish are mollusks too, but they have no shell. The eight-armed octopus uses its suckered tentacles to catch crabs and other animals for food. By shooting water through a built-in nozzle, the octopus swims through water at high speed.

gill: structure on fish and certain other animals for extracting dissolved oxygen from water.

mollusk: type of marine invertebrate, often having a shell. [MOL-usk]

Construction and development have changed much of North America's coastline. But many areas remain protected as parks or refuges. If you visit a coastal area, enjoy its natural beauty.

CORAL REEFS

Coral polyps are tiny animals with soft, transparent bodies. They build rocky outer skeletons around their bodies. When the polyp dies, the skeleton remains. Other coral polyps grow on top. Over thousands of years, the leftover skeletons build a coral reef.

Coral reefs grow only in warm seas. Scientists have found them offshore in the Caribbean Sea and the Red Sea, near Mexico and Latin America, and off the shores of South America and Africa. Coral reefs also grow offshore in the South Pacific and near Southeast Asia.

Stretching 1,200 miles (1,920 km) offshore from northeast Australia, the Great Barrier Reef is the world's largest coral reef. It began forming over 30 million years ago and covers an area roughly as big as Kansas.

More than 400 species of coral live on the Great Barrier Reef. Brain coral formations look like squiggly plastic models of a brain. Staghorn coral formations resemble deer antlers. Still other coral branches outward in feathery wisps. Some corals are pink. Others are red. Still others are bright yellow or orange.

Coral reefs attract many sea animals. Many feed on the tiny polyps themselves. Others find prey swimming along in the reef. These fishes, sea anemones, sea stars, and other creatures often have brilliant colors.

Coral reefs are beautiful, but fragile. Severe tropical storms can devastate large reef areas. Overfishing, pollution, and too much diving can also disturb the fragile ecology.

DEEP, DEEP DOWN

Most of the ocean floor is dark and desolate. But scientists have found some amazing organisms living kilometers below the surface near deep sea vents. These vents are like underwater chimneys, venting heat from Earth's hot interior.

Microscopic **archaeons** are the oddest of these organisms. When scientists studied the genes of one microscopic archaeon, it was different from anything they had ever seen. The scientists decided to declare a new kingdom of organisms—archaea.

Other bizarre sea vent creatures include giant tube worms, giant foot-long (30 cm) clams, and huge mussels. Needless to say, the discoveries surprised scientists in the 1970s and 1980s. "Imagine being in a desert in the bottom of the ocean and coming upon an oasis," says Rutgers University biologist Bob Vrijenhoek, "except now it was covered with giant tube worms and all sorts of things that no one had any idea about at first." Scientists are still finding new life deep down in the ocean.

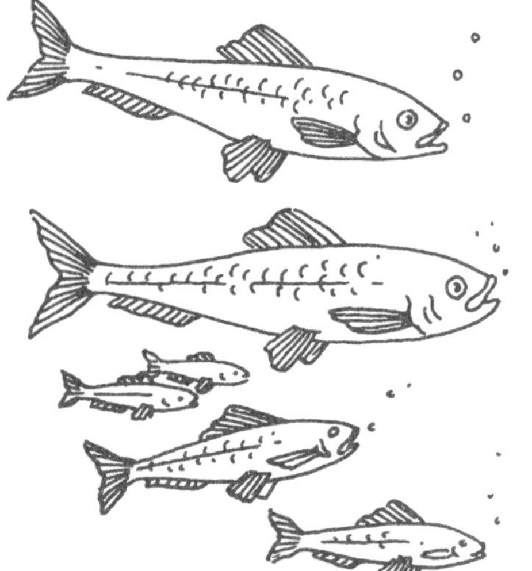

RIVERS, LAKES, AND STREAMS

North America's thousands of rivers, lakes, and streams teem with life. Rushes and sedges growing near banks have hard stalks and broad, cornlike leaves. Water lilies' stems and roots grow underwater, but their leaves (pads) and flowers float on top. Other plants, like the wispy Ceratophylla, live completely submerged.

Freshwater fishes include salmon, trout, minnows, and more. Frogs, salamanders, newts, snails, diving spiders, and water fleas also make their homes in and near water. Dragonflies, mosquitoes, and other insects thrive here too.

Next time you swim, boat, or fish on a lake or river, enjoy these beautiful watery areas. And keep an eye open for the life that abounds in these freshwater habitats.

WORDS to KNOW

archaeon: single-celled organism found near deep sea vents. [ar-KAY-on]

Featured Creature

Sea Stars

Sea stars aren't at all like outer space stars. Sea stars, sometimes called starfish, belong to a group of invertebrates called **echinoderms**. The word means "spiny skins." The spiny skins protect sea stars' soft bodies underneath.

Your body has a left side and a right side. Sea stars and other echinoderms, like sea urchins and sea cucumbers, have radial bodies. Like spokes of a wheel, their bodies are arranged in sections around a middle part. Most of the 3,600 kinds of sea stars have 5 "arms," or rays. Some have as many as 20 rays!

Sea stars' middles contain their mouth, guts, and various other body parts. Tube feet poke out from their underside. The tube feet move the animal along underwater shores and tidal pools as it searches for clams, oysters, and other food.

If a sea star's arm breaks off during another animal's attack, it can regrow, or **regenerate**, the arm. Basically, the sea star's cells can reproduce and specialize to replace the arm with all its features. But the growth takes time. If you find a starfish at the shore, gently return it unharmed to the water.

WORDS to KNOW

echinoderm: spiny-skinned sea animal, such as a sea star. [ee-KINE-oh-derm]

regenerate: regrow. [ree-JEN-er-ATE]

WETLANDS

Covered with water for at least part of the year, **wetlands** may seem smelly and stagnant. But marshes, swamps, and bogs play important roles in nature.

Water-loving grasses, rushes, and sedges are the dominant plants in marshes. Cattails, water lilies, duckweed, and water hyacinths are common too. Great egrets, swamp rabbits, alligators, and red-eared turtles are just a few animals that make marshes their home.

Besides providing a home for animals, marsh plants help control pollution. They help filter certain chemicals out of the water. Other plants remove microscopic organisms that could trigger disease.

Swamps have many water-loving trees and shrubs. Cypress trees stand tall in swamps in Louisiana, Florida, South Carolina, and elsewhere. Mangrove trees tower in coastal swamps in Florida and other southeastern states. They protect the shore from destructive storms.

Peatlands are another kind of wetlands. Sphagnum moss in bogs produces energy-rich peat.

Some peatlands also provide a home to the carnivorous pitcher plant. Rainwater collects in the plant's tall, cup-shaped leaves. Bright colors near the rim and a nectar scent attract insects. Once inside, the insects can't climb up the cup's slippery walls to escape. Bacteria and enzymes in the cup decompose the insects after they drown. Then the pitcher plant uses the nutrients for food.

Two hundred years ago, the United States had about 2 million acres of wetlands. Barely half of that remains today. Fortunately, Congress has passed laws to halt future losses. By restricting dredging, filling, and other activities, the law aims to protect America's wetland habitats.

wetlands: areas that are covered by water all or part of the year, or which are characterized by certain types of organisms.

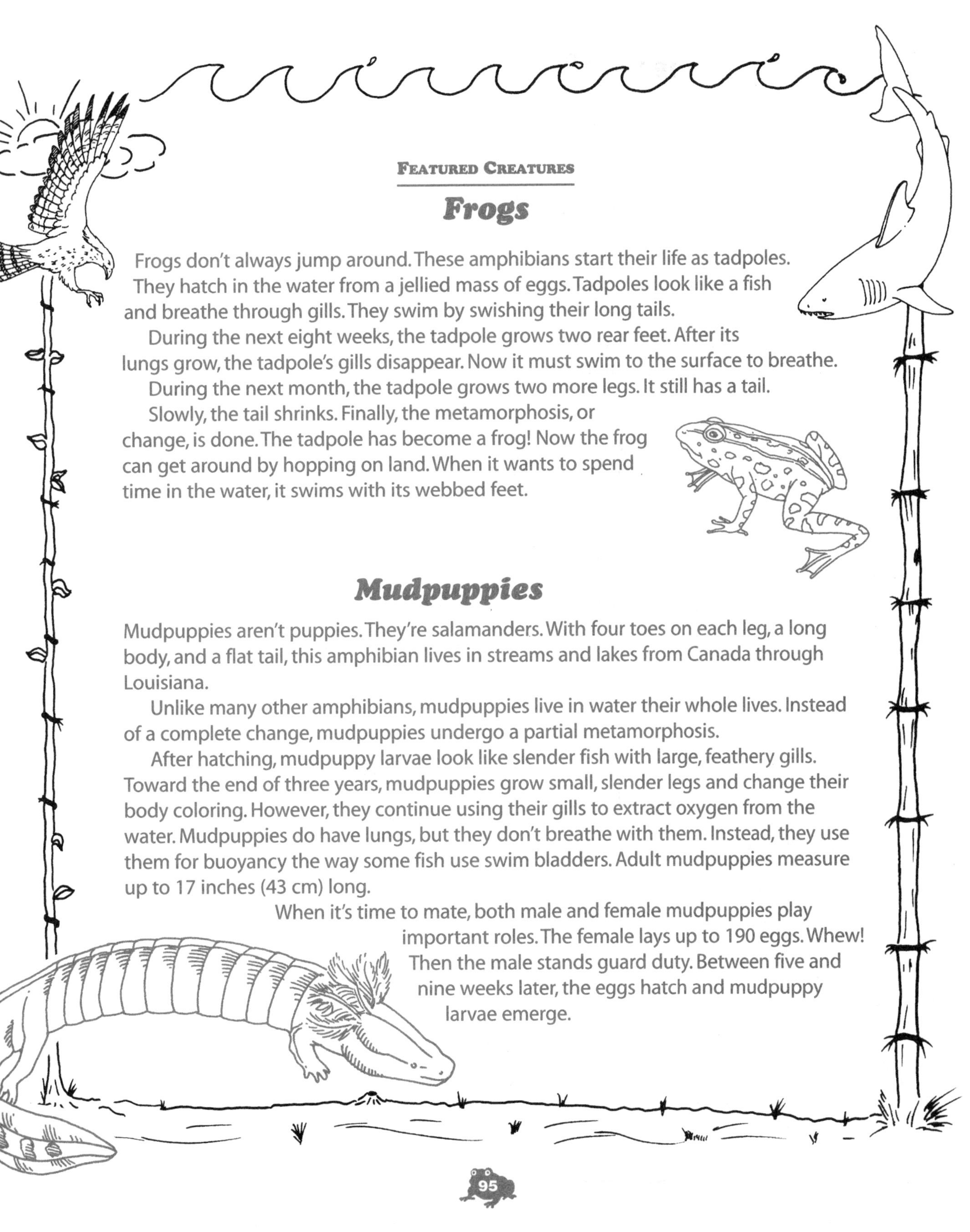

Frogs

Frogs don't always jump around. These amphibians start their life as tadpoles. They hatch in the water from a jellied mass of eggs. Tadpoles look like a fish and breathe through gills. They swim by swishing their long tails.

During the next eight weeks, the tadpole grows two rear feet. After its lungs grow, the tadpole's gills disappear. Now it must swim to the surface to breathe.

During the next month, the tadpole grows two more legs. It still has a tail.

Slowly, the tail shrinks. Finally, the metamorphosis, or change, is done. The tadpole has become a frog! Now the frog can get around by hopping on land. When it wants to spend time in the water, it swims with its webbed feet.

Mudpuppies

Mudpuppies aren't puppies. They're salamanders. With four toes on each leg, a long body, and a flat tail, this amphibian lives in streams and lakes from Canada through Louisiana.

Unlike many other amphibians, mudpuppies live in water their whole lives. Instead of a complete change, mudpuppies undergo a partial metamorphosis.

After hatching, mudpuppy larvae look like slender fish with large, feathery gills. Toward the end of three years, mudpuppies grow small, slender legs and change their body coloring. However, they continue using their gills to extract oxygen from the water. Mudpuppies do have lungs, but they don't breathe with them. Instead, they use them for buoyancy the way some fish use swim bladders. Adult mudpuppies measure up to 17 inches (43 cm) long.

When it's time to mate, both male and female mudpuppies play important roles. The female lays up to 190 eggs. Whew! Then the male stands guard duty. Between five and nine weeks later, the eggs hatch and mudpuppy larvae emerge.

FEATURED CREATURE

Alligators

How can you tell an alligator from a crocodile? Both live in marshes and swamps, and both look somewhat alike. But there are differences.

An alligator's snout is broad and U-shaped. The crocodile's snout is narrow and pointed. Alligators are dark-colored. Crocodiles are grayish green.

Also, with its mouth shut, the alligator's teeth are all hidden. Two of the crocodile's teeth stick out even when its jaws are closed.

Just don't get too close to those jaws. Alligators can snap their jaws shut with up to 1,200 pounds of force per square inch! Fishes, turtles, or other prey make tasty alligator meals.

Alligators are cold-blooded. Their body temperatures match the surrounding temperature. To get warm, they move into the sun. To cool off, they seek the shade or rest underwater.

A transparent membrane protects its eyes but still lets the alligator see when it's underwater.

Adult alligators hiss and bellow, especially during mating season. After mating, the female lays up to 70 eggs in a nest on shore. Then she piles soil, grass, and leaves on top of them.

The rotting plants not only hide the eggs, but also give off heat that helps them hatch. Although she doesn't "sit" on the nest, the mother watches over her nest from nearby in the water.

CHAPTER 9
PEOPLE AFFECTING NATURE

GIVE A HOOT ABOUT HABITAT LOSS

For decades, America's logging industry has clashed with environmentalists. Loggers wanted to cut down more trees. Environmentalists wanted to protect the spotted owl's home.

The spotted owl only lives in "ancient" forests with trees 100 to 200 years old. Once 15 million acres of ancient forests covered parts of North America. Now 90 percent of that has been cut down.

Unlike "new" plantation-style forests, ancient forests have uneven tree growth. Fallen logs, dead tree remains, and certain kinds of fungi attract flying squirrels and other animals. They, in turn, become the spotted owl's prey.

The spotted owl was listed as "threatened" under the United States' Endangered Species Act. While the spotted owl has legal protection, its long-term survival remains a hotly debated issue.

THE SPECTER OF SPRAWL

Habitat loss also occurs as cities and suburbs expand. **Sprawl** is the spread of cities and suburbs to rural areas. On one hand, more space for people to live seems like a good idea. Left uncontrolled, however, sprawl destroys forests and crowds out wildlife.

sprawl: growth of urban and suburban areas into formerly rural areas.

Sprawl has public health costs too. More traffic and congestion means more pollution. Also, crowding could mean more contact with certain animal-transmitted diseases.

Groups like the Sierra Club and American Forests want to stop sprawl. Building

in existing urban areas, they say, reduces further loss of natural areas.

Keep an ear open to learn what building is planned in your community. Find out how developers want to address environmental concerns. Let your local leaders know how you feel.

Areas that are already developed need help too. Tree planting can give nature a big boost in these areas. They can attract nesting birds and other species back. That helps make the neighborhood nicer for everyone.

Trees are cool—literally. Trees shade buildings during hot summers. This reduces energy needs for air conditioning. Trees keep areas cooler too by releasing water vapor through their leaves. This process is called transpiration.

It's a Natural Fact!

Six Billion and Growing

On October 12, 1999, Earth's population reached six billion people. Meeting everyone's needs while conserving natural resources is a prime challenge for the twenty-first century.

Get Active!

Party Favor Trees

The next time you host a party, why not give trees as party favors? Your friends can have fun planting them, and you'll all help the environment.

Depending on when your party is held, you may be able to root cuttings from one of your family's own trees. About two weeks before the party, plant each cutting in a large paper cup filled with potting soil. Set the cups in a lighted place. Keep the soil damp. Soon the cuttings should grow roots.

You can also get small trees by mail. The National Arbor Day Foundation offers 10 trees in return for a membership donation. Contact them at 100 Arbor Avenue, Nebraska City, NE 68410. Their Web site is *http://www.arborday.org*.

Trees also control stormwater runoff and prevent erosion. That's a big help because concrete can't soak up rainwater the way soil does. Some trees even filter certain pollutants out of the air. In short, trees benefit us and our urban and suburban environments in lots of ways.

ALIEN INVADERS

Americans first saw kudzu at the 1876 Centennial Exposition. The Exposition was a huge fair. Countries from around the world set up exhibits. Visitors loved the kudzu vine's lavender-blue flowers and its sweet grape-like scent at the Japanese pavilion.

Soon kudzu seemed to be everywhere. People bought the vines for their homes. Farmers fed it to livestock. The Soil Conservation Service told people to use it to prevent erosion—the washing away of soil by water.

Kudzu had fewer natural enemies in America than it did in Japan, and it adapted amazingly well to its new home. Now kudzu covers more than 2 million acres in the South. Each plant grows up to 100 feet (30 m) per year.

This is good for kudzu, but bad for other species. Invading kudzu uses resources that native species need to survive. And vines can quickly cover buildings, bridges, and even power lines. No wonder some people call kudzu "the vine that ate the South!"

Kudzu isn't the only **alien** invader. The Australian melaleuca tree made itself right at home in Florida's Everglades. The 70-foot (21 m) tall trees crowd out tall saw-grass in the marshes. Then wildlife that depends on the sawgrass suffers too.

Tamarisk is a woody plant from areas around the Mediterranean Sea. Starting

WORDS to KNOW

alien: not native to a specific habitat; foreign. [ALE-ee-en]

pesticide: product designed to kill harmful insects or other organisms. [PESS-tih-side]

bioaccumulate: process by which poisons travel through the food chain from one species to another. [BYE-oh-ah-KYOOM-yoo-late]

Featured Creature

Peregrine Falcons

Peregrine falcons almost became extinct. Now these birds are making a comeback.

Soaring gracefully through the air, peregrine falcons search for songbirds, pigeons, quail, or other small birds. Peregrines are a kind of bird called raptors—sharp-clawed birds that hunt other animals for food. Their preferred habitat is high cliffs above open country.

With keen eyesight, a peregrine targets its prey. Then it swiftly swoops, or dives down, at speeds up to 200 miles per hour (320 km/h). With powerful talons, the peregrine snaps up its quarry in midair. The peregrine flies to a rocky cliff. A hooked notch on its beak lets the peregrine kill and tear apart its meaty meal.

A typical female weighs about two pounds (1 kg) and has a wingspan of 45 inches (115 cm). Males, called tiercels, are about a third smaller than females.

Male and female peregrines mate for life. Often they return to the same nest, or eyrie, to raise their young.

Years ago, several thousand peregrines roamed North America. Then the numbers dwindled to almost nothing. Scientists finally discovered that DDT was to blame.

DDT was a **pesticide** used from the 1940s through the 1960s. When small birds ate insects sprayed with DDT, the chemical stayed in their system. Peregrines ate the small birds, and DDT got into their bodies. Chemicals traveling through the food chain this way are said to **bioaccumulate.**

DDT made the peregrines' egg shells too soft. Without protection from a hard shell, developing peregrines perished. In 1972, the United States and other countries made DDT illegal.

But people still worried about the peregrines. Scientists at Cornell University and elsewhere began captive breeding programs. Using incubators, scientists hatched baby peregrines. They used puppets to train the babies as if they were in the wild. Then, when the babies were grown, scientists released them into the wild. Thanks to the breeding programs, the United States had about 875 pairs of peregrines by the mid-1990s.

Today if you are in cliff country, you may see graceful peregrines soar through the air. You may also see peregrines in cities like Cleveland, New York, Ottawa, and Toronto. When scientists released them, some peregrines decided that they liked living on the artificial "cliffs" of tall skyscrapers. This is a good example of behavioral adaptation. More peregrines survive, and more people get to see these magnificent birds.

in the nineteenth century, people planted tamarisk in the southwestern United States to control erosion. Now spreading tamarisk has invaded many areas of White Sands National Monument in New Mexico. As tamarisk forms dense thickets, it soaks up water that native plants need.

ballast: water a ship carries so it floats at the right level. [BAL-ast]

Animals can be invaders too. In the 1980s, zebra mussels accidentally got a free ride to North America inside ship **ballast**. Ballast is water that a ship carries so it floats at the right level. The zebra mussels made their way to the Great Lakes. With few natural enemies, they grew on every hard surface they could find, including pipes, boats, and docks. By 1995, people had spent over $120 million responding to the damage.

In July 1998, Asian longhorned beetles invaded Chicago, Illinois. By August 1999, the white and black bugs besieged areas in New York City and Long Island. Larvae (young beetles) eat through tree trunks and branches. The holes keep water from flowing through the tree. The tree dies, and then the beetles infest another tree. No one knows where the invasion might spread next.

Not all foreign species are bad. Soybeans, wheat, and cattle were not native to the United States. They now play a major role in American agriculture.

Many popular garden plants were also brought to North America from other countries. Colorful spring tulips, for example, first came from Europe and Asia. Daffodils first grew near the Mediterranean Sea.

But people can't always predict the future. What seems pretty today could well become the kudzu weed of tomorrow.

After habitat destruction, The Nature Conservancy says the next biggest threat to species survival

comes from non-native species. The federal government is developing a plan to address problems from non-native species. Even if they're not from outer space, alien invaders are a real problem.

ENDANGERED SPECIES

Billions (literally!) of passenger pigeons once flew across North America. Then too many people killed the birds for food or sport. As many as 700,000 birds died each month during the early nineteenth century. The species could not recover. The world's last passenger pigeon, named Martha, died in 1914 at the Cincinnati Zoo.

Sadly, hundreds of plants and animals are still threatened with extinction. Whooping cranes, grizzly bears, Florida manatees, Wyoming toads, sea turtles, and hundreds of other species are in a very vulnerable position.

Much of nature's beauty lies in the wide variety of life found on Earth. Beyond this, the loss of any species can have unforeseen consequences on the balance of nature in its habitat. Organisms that depended on a species for food, pollination, seed dispersal, or other functions could also become endangered. Finally, scientists have developed many medicines from nature's resources. No one knows

GET ACTIVE!

Speed Swooping

See for yourself how a compact diving shape helps peregrines catch their prey.

You need:
two sheets 8-½″ x 11″ paper
transparent tape
ladder or sturdy chair
CAUTION: Use caution when climbing on anything. Ask an adult to supervise.

1. Hold each sheet of paper horizontally and fold it into accordion pleats about ¾″ wide.
2. Tape each sheet around one end to make a fan.
3. Tape the pleats of one sheet together at the other end. Leave the other sheet fanned out.
4. Carefully climb on a small ladder or sturdy chair. Then drop them. Which seems to move faster?

Taping the pleats together on one paper reduced its wind resistance. In the same way, peregrines reduce their wind resistance by tucking in their wings and diving head first to make a kill.

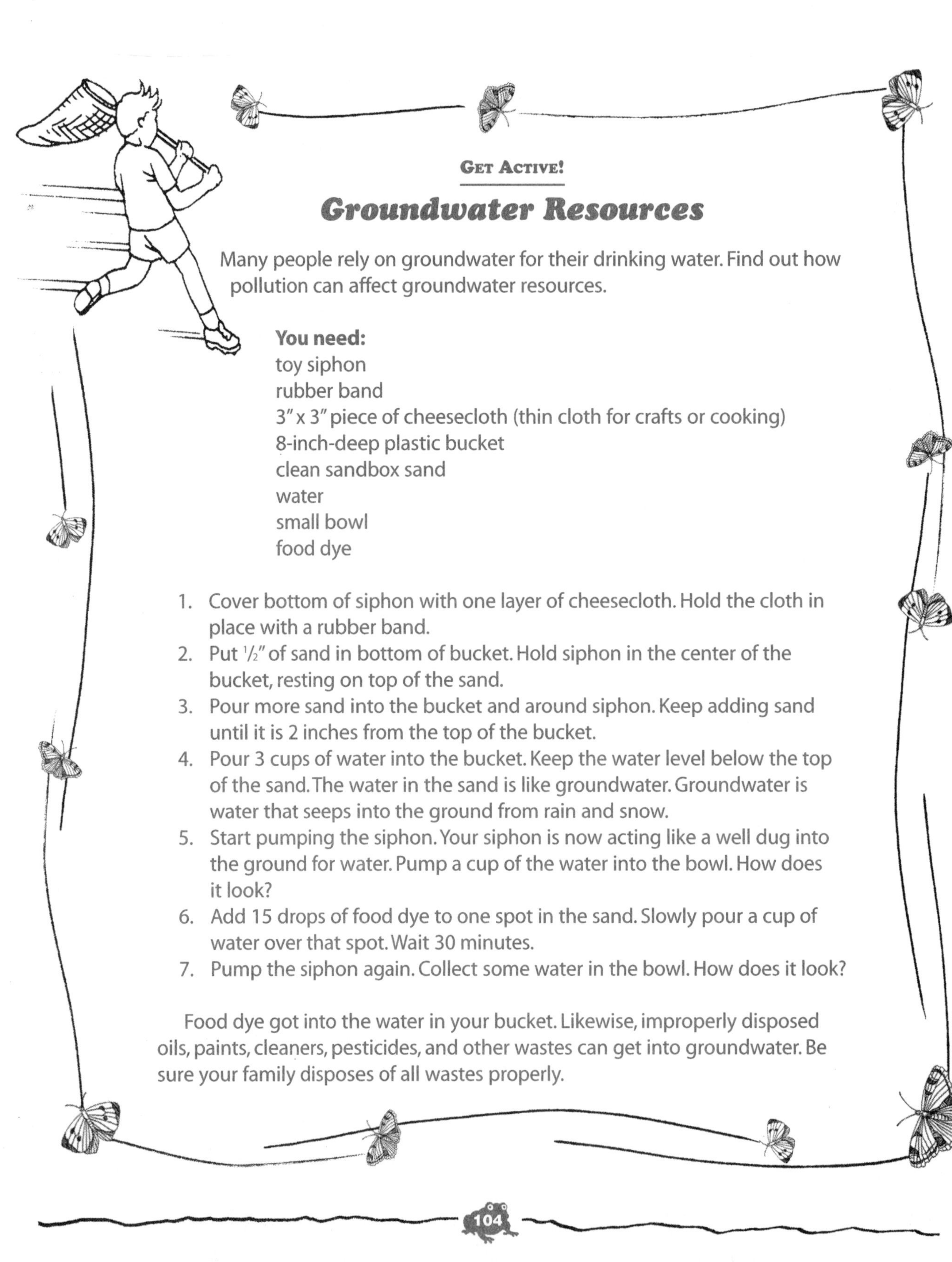

GET ACTIVE!

Groundwater Resources

Many people rely on groundwater for their drinking water. Find out how pollution can affect groundwater resources.

You need:
toy siphon
rubber band
3″ x 3″ piece of cheesecloth (thin cloth for crafts or cooking)
8-inch-deep plastic bucket
clean sandbox sand
water
small bowl
food dye

1. Cover bottom of siphon with one layer of cheesecloth. Hold the cloth in place with a rubber band.
2. Put ½″ of sand in bottom of bucket. Hold siphon in the center of the bucket, resting on top of the sand.
3. Pour more sand into the bucket and around siphon. Keep adding sand until it is 2 inches from the top of the bucket.
4. Pour 3 cups of water into the bucket. Keep the water level below the top of the sand. The water in the sand is like groundwater. Groundwater is water that seeps into the ground from rain and snow.
5. Start pumping the siphon. Your siphon is now acting like a well dug into the ground for water. Pump a cup of the water into the bowl. How does it look?
6. Add 15 drops of food dye to one spot in the sand. Slowly pour a cup of water over that spot. Wait 30 minutes.
7. Pump the siphon again. Collect some water in the bowl. How does it look?

Food dye got into the water in your bucket. Likewise, improperly disposed oils, paints, cleaners, pesticides, and other wastes can get into groundwater. Be sure your family disposes of all wastes properly.

whether an extinct species may have given us a cure for cancer, AIDS, or other serious illnesses.

Fortunately, the United States, Canada, and other countries have laws to protect threatened and endangered species. Treaties and research programs also seek to promote species survival. Let's hope these programs to protect threatened and endangered species succeed.

POLLUTION PROBLEMS

Air, water, and soil pollution can cause serious health problems for people. Pollution can also have devastating effects on nature.

In 1989, the *Exxon Valdez* oil tanker ran into a rocky reef off Alaska's south shore. It spilled over 10 million gallons (44 million liters) of oil into the sea. Despite a clean-up costing more than $1 billion, thousands of birds, sea otters, and other animals died. Other animals, like herring, hatched young with birth defects.

Other types of water pollution can also cause problems. Scientists and environmental regulators believe that deformed fishes in various rivers were poisoned by wastewater discharges. Some discharges come from factories or sewers. Others come from fertilizer and roadway runoff.

Laws now regulate what companies and cities can discharge into water bodies. They also closely control air emissions and other kinds of waste disposal. The laws have made a big difference in protecting the environment for people and other species.

ACID RAIN

What happens when sulfur dioxide and nitrogen dioxide emissions travel hundreds of miles? Dissolved in water vapor, they can cause rain and other precipitation to be far more acidic than normal. This problem is called **acid rain**.

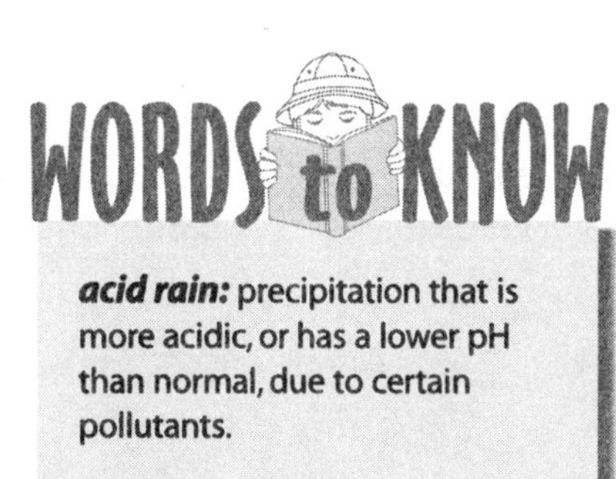

acid rain: precipitation that is more acidic, or has a lower pH than normal, due to certain pollutants.

Trees at the top of North Carolina's Mount Mitchell look dead and barren. Scientists believe that the effects of acid rain and bugs called woolly adelgids combined to devastate the trees. Forests in Europe have also been ravaged by acid rain.

Acid rain also pollutes lakes and streams. Some lakes are now so acidic that fish can't live in them.

GLOBAL WARMING

Global warming may not seem like a bad idea when you're shivering on a winter day. But scientists warn that a gradual warming of Earth's temperature could mean ecological disaster.

Carbon dioxide and other gases are given off when people burn fuel, drive cars, and do various other activities. Cutting down and burning areas of forest also releases gases to the air.

Over time, these gases can produce a "greenhouse effect." The glass of a greenhouse traps the sun's heat inside, so that it's much warmer than the air outside—just like a car gets hot when the windows are closed on a sunny day.

In the same way, scientists say greenhouse gases trap more of the sun's heat in

GET ACTIVE!

Time to Clean Up

Walking through the woods is not nearly as much fun if empty bottles and papers litter the trail. And playing at the beach gets gross when cigarette butts and other trash mix with the sand.

Do your part to help clean up our act. During April, many groups sponsor park clean-ups for Earth Day. In September, other groups plan beach clean-ups. Also, throughout the year, many clubs have Adopt-a-Highway programs where members clean debris along stretches of roadways.

You can also get a clean-up group going yourself. Ask local environmental groups or your department of health for advice and safety tips, such as wearing gloves. Then recruit friends in Scout troops, classes, or clubs. Always bring an adult along for safety and supervision.

the **atmosphere**. Natural events, such as volcanic eruptions, can also cause temporary warming until clouds of volcanic ash settle.

By the turn of the next century, global temperatures could rise up to 6°F (3.5°C). Some of the rise may be natural, but some is likely due to people's activities.

Scientists worry that even that seemingly small rise could cause catastrophes. Hurricanes, typhoons, droughts, and other weather disasters could become much more severe. Meanwhile, melting even small amounts of polar ice could cause massive flooding.

Scientists concerned about global warming urge people to reduce greenhouse gases and stop cutting down forest areas. That way, they say, less carbon dioxide will build up in the atmosphere.

WORDS to KNOW

atmosphere: layers of air surrounding Earth from its surface up to space. [AT-moss-fear]

FIGHT GREENHOUSE GASES

Here are five simple things you can do to reduce greenhouse gases.

1. Walk places with your friends and family instead of driving all the time.
2. Too far to walk? Try public transportation.
3. When you do travel by car, share rides with friends. Your parents will save driving time too.
4. Recycle materials at home. You'll save money and reduce energy demands needed to make new products.
5. Turn off lights when you leave a room.

CHAPTER 10
ENJOY THE GREAT OUTDOORS

TAKE A HIKE!

Get your exercise and enjoy nature at the same time. Hike in a park or nature area near home.

Hiking offers year-round fun. See summer sunlight streaming through tall trees. Listen to the crunch of autumn leaves underfoot. Watch winter ice glisten on frozen lakes. Breathe in sweet smells after a spring rain.

Here are some hiking essentials:

A buddy. Safety comes first. Never hike alone. Bring an adult along for safety.

Shoes. On flat, dry ground, sneakers work fine. If the weather's wet, wear waterproof boots. Cold, muddy toes are no fun.

If you hike a lot in wilderness areas, you may need hiking boots. Their design supports you on rough terrain.

Clothes. Of course, you'll wear clothes. You don't need designer duds, but do dress smartly.

Think layers. If you start warming up, take off one sweatshirt. Or, if the day gets cooler, add a windbreaker. (Having a water-repellent jacket is an added plus in case of rain.)

Dress to avoid dangers too. Stay away from areas with lots of poison ivy, mosquitoes, or ticks. If there may be even a few of these pests, wear pants and a long-sleeved shirt. They protect you better than a tank top and shorts.

Insect repellent and sunscreen. Bug bites are a bummer. Use insect repellents to avoid itchy areas later. Wear sunscreen too.

Trail maps. Many parks have trail maps. Most tell you how long each path is and if it's easy or hard. Easy trails tend to be short and level.

IT'S A NATURAL FACT!

Hug a Tree

If you get lost on a hike, hug a tree. It sounds silly, but it helps.

For one thing, hugging a tree keeps you in one place. Shout out or blow your whistle periodically to help searchers find you.

Also, unless there's a thunderstorm, the tree provides some shelter. (If there is a thunderstorm, get away from trees, crouch low, and balance on the balls of your feet until the lightning passes.)

Hard trails may be steep or rocky. Check whether the path loops back to where you started. If not, allow time to double back.

Even if you're just hiking through the neighborhood, have a map in your mind and know where you're going. Getting lost is no fun.

Safety supplies. Bring along some basic first aid supplies, like Band-Aids, antiseptic, and an ace bandage. Carry a small flashlight and a whistle, too, in case you encounter trouble along the way and need to summon help.

Snacks. Trail mix, granola bars, or sandwiches are fun foods for hikes. It's especially important to bring a filled water bottle or canteen. Pack up all trash and carry it out with you.

Knapsack or fannypack. An inexpensive pack helps you carry all this stuff easily.

HIKES AWAY FROM HOME

Is your family going on vacation? Hikes are a great way to discover nature in another part of the country or a different part of the world. And hikes make a welcome change from crowded tourist spots.

Get guidebooks about your destination from a bookstore or library. Also write to the local visitor's bureau about a month before leaving. Ask for maps and recommendations for kid-friendly hikes.

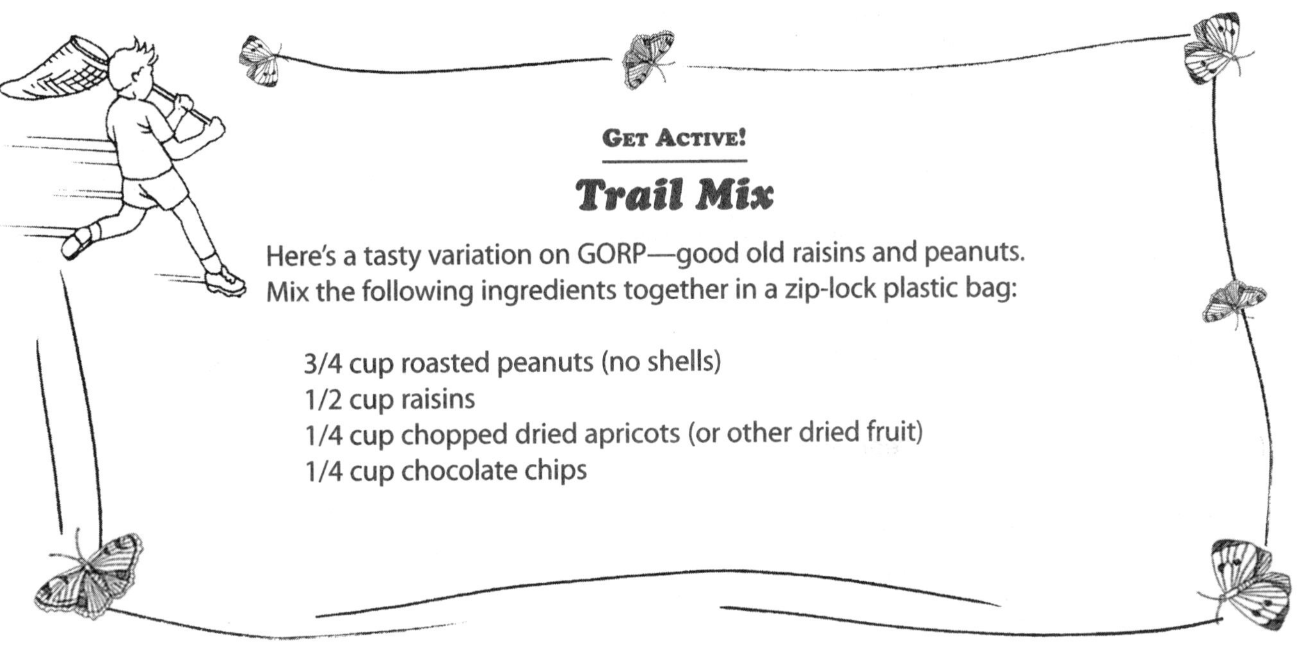

GET ACTIVE!

Trail Mix

Here's a tasty variation on GORP—good old raisins and peanuts. Mix the following ingredients together in a zip-lock plastic bag:

3/4 cup roasted peanuts (no shells)
1/2 cup raisins
1/4 cup chopped dried apricots (or other dried fruit)
1/4 cup chocolate chips

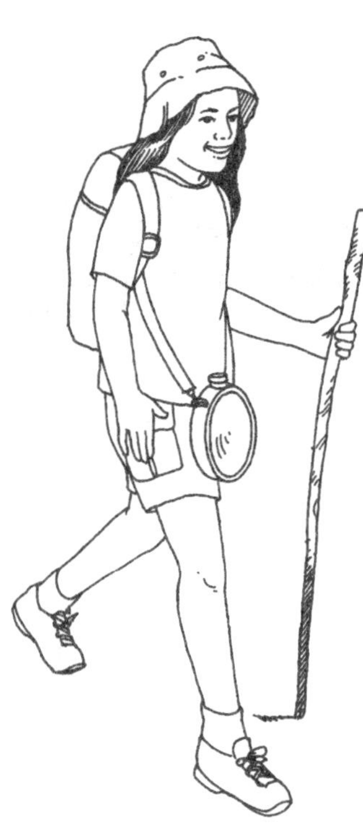

Here are some cool hiking spots to visit in the United States:

Diamond Head. Start inside this extinct volcano on the island of Oahu in Hawaii. Hike up and enjoy the view; then come back down.

Mount Ranier. This snow-covered volcano in Washington State has trails snaking through forest-covered areas. Warmer areas are at the lower altitudes. Temperatures get cooler as you travel up. The mountain's peak is snow-covered year round.

Grand Canyon. Hike down into the canyon and enjoy magnificent views. Allow twice as much time to walk back up.

Rocky Mountain National Park. Located near Estes Park, Colorado, this park's trails range from easy to challenging. At higher altitudes you can see alpine tundra.

Buckeye Trail. Blue blazes on trees mark the trail. It follows a triangular path through Ohio.

Mountains to Seas Trail. This series of hiking trails takes you through beautiful areas in North Carolina.

Freedom Trail. This urban trail winds through Boston, Massachusetts. Start at Boston Commons, a pretty downtown park. Then follow the trail to landmarks in American history.

CAMPOUTS

Discover nature with a campout. If you live in a suburb or rural area, start by hosting a tent sleep-over in your back yard. Set up the tent before it gets dark. Make sure you have strong flashlights in case anyone needs to head back to the house at night.

Want to venture farther than the back yard?

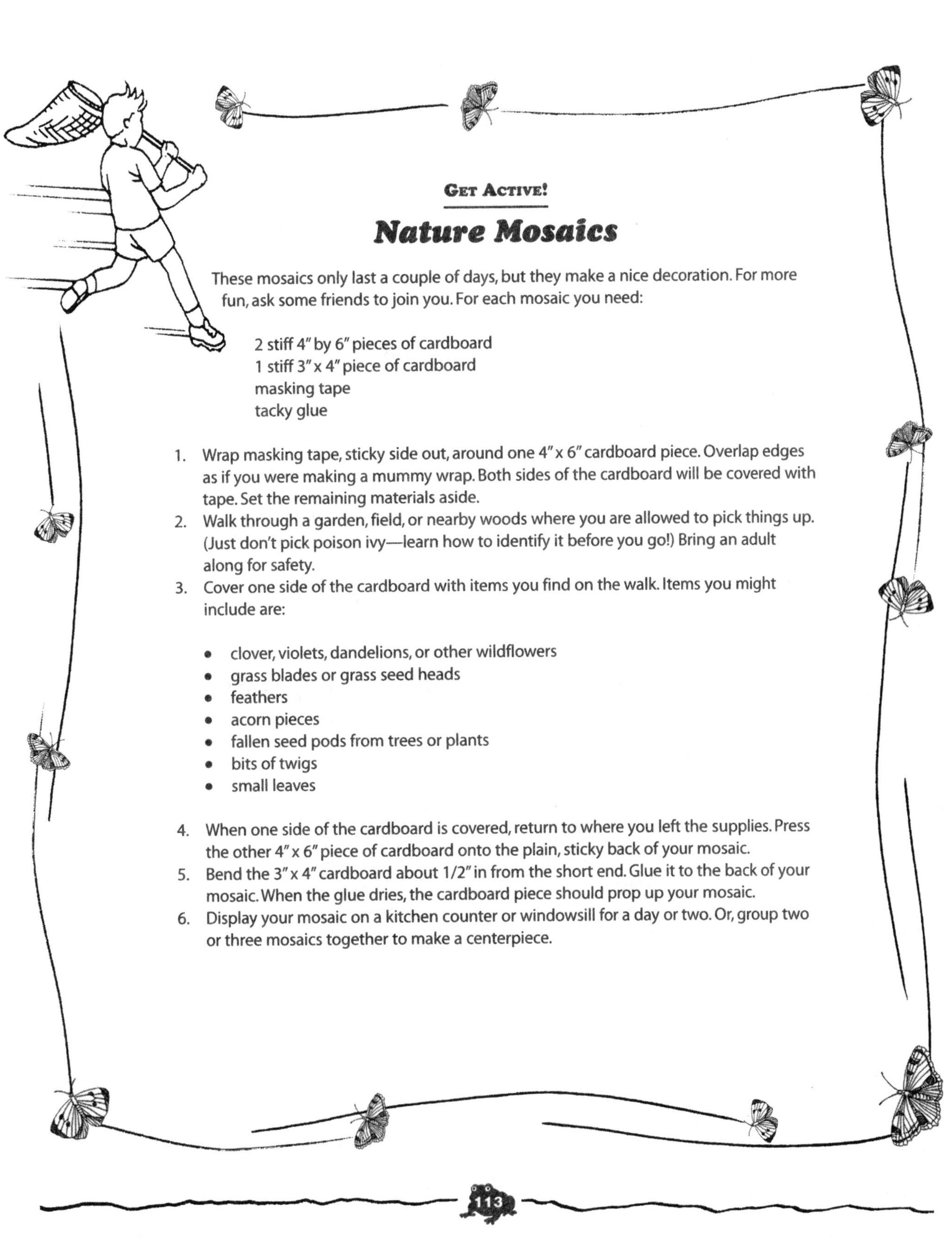

GET ACTIVE!

Nature Mosaics

These mosaics only last a couple of days, but they make a nice decoration. For more fun, ask some friends to join you. For each mosaic you need:

2 stiff 4″ by 6″ pieces of cardboard
1 stiff 3″ x 4″ piece of cardboard
masking tape
tacky glue

1. Wrap masking tape, sticky side out, around one 4″ x 6″ cardboard piece. Overlap edges as if you were making a mummy wrap. Both sides of the cardboard will be covered with tape. Set the remaining materials aside.
2. Walk through a garden, field, or nearby woods where you are allowed to pick things up. (Just don't pick poison ivy—learn how to identify it before you go!) Bring an adult along for safety.
3. Cover one side of the cardboard with items you find on the walk. Items you might include are:

   - clover, violets, dandelions, or other wildflowers
   - grass blades or grass seed heads
   - feathers
   - acorn pieces
   - fallen seed pods from trees or plants
   - bits of twigs
   - small leaves

4. When one side of the cardboard is covered, return to where you left the supplies. Press the other 4″ x 6″ piece of cardboard onto the plain, sticky back of your mosaic.
5. Bend the 3″ x 4″ cardboard about 1/2″ in from the short end. Glue it to the back of your mosaic. When the glue dries, the cardboard piece should prop up your mosaic.
6. Display your mosaic on a kitchen counter or windowsill for a day or two. Or, group two or three mosaics together to make a centerpiece.

Groups like the Girl Scouts and Boy Scouts of America and the YMCA have campgrounds throughout the country. Contact chapters near you for more information.

You can also try camping with your family on vacation. Many federal and state parks welcome campers. But campsites fill up early. Plan early—as much as a year in advance!

ART IN NATURE

Sunlight dances among the tree leaves. Mountains rise majestically. Shadows stretch across the desert in the late afternoon.

Nature has inspired artists for centuries. Let its beauty help you express your own artistic talent. Get a sturdy clipboard and some basic art materials together. Then head outside and have fun sketching or painting with any or all of these media:

- Charcoal
- Colored pencils
- Crayons
- Pastels
- Watercolor paints
- Oil paints

NATURE PHOTOGRAPHY

Nature photography starts with a camera, plus some film. Start by learning how your camera works. Know how to load film, how to hold the camera, and how to snap the shutter without "camera shake." You want photos of nature—not shaky blurs!

You'll be outside, so be sure to protect your camera. Use the wrist or neck strap to avoid dropping the camera. Keep the camera dry by bringing along a waterproof, padded camera bag.

Sometimes you want photos, but you don't want to risk getting your own camera wet or sandy. A rainy day walk or trip to the seashore may be just the time to try a disposable waterproof camera.

Take pictures of what appeals to you. Here are some ideas:

Plants. Take photos to show the range of plants in an area. How many can you name offhand? Look up the others in a field guide after your pictures are developed.

Another idea is to focus your photo session on just one plant. Photograph it from different perspectives. If you're shooting a cactus, for example, photograph the whole plant. Then zoom in on its needles or a flower.

Wildlife. See how many animals you can snap with your camera. Tread softly so you won't scare off your subject.

Mountains. Take one broad, scenic shot. Ask a friend to stand in the picture as a "ruler" to show just how big other items are. Also take several shots in a series. Piece them together later to make an interesting collage.

Water. Crashing waves, babbling brooks, and a mirror-like lake are all great photo subjects.

Sunrise and sunset. Check the newspaper in advance to see what time the sun will rise or set. Then get to your spot early so you won't miss the moment.

GET ACTIVE!

Keep a Nature Journal

Express your love of nature by keeping a journal. Buy a decorated blank book, or just write in a plain notebook. Either way, make sure you like the journal and can carry it easily.

Find somewhere comfortable to do your writing. It can be under a back yard tree, on the front porch, or by a window with a pretty view. Perhaps you prefer a bench at the park or a sandy spot near the sea.

Take your journal along when you travel too. Write about nature in different places.

You don't have to write a lot each time. Just write as much as you want. The idea is to have fun.

What should you write? That's up to you. Here are some ideas to get you started:

- Describe the scene before you. What do you see? What sounds do you hear? What scents do you smell? Is it warm or cold? Is the air breezy or still?
- Focus on a single part of nature. What kind of tree are you sitting under? How does the grass feel and smell? How does the squirrel act as it scampers by?
- Find metaphors and similes in nature. A simile is a comparison using "like" or "as." For example: "The snow drifted against the fence like daubs of whipped cream."

  A metaphor says something *is* what you're comparing it to. For example: "The moss is a velvety green carpet on the forest floor."
- Find inspiration in nature. Sunlight outlining a dark cloud may make you feel hopeful. Dancing shadows of leaves may seem playful. Even a weed pushing through a sidewalk crack can show determination and a will to survive.

Color cues. Focusing on one color helps train your eye to take photos. Pick a color like green, red, yellow, or brown. What different things can you find in nature that feature your color?

Black and white scenes. Famous photographer Ansel Adams took beautiful black and white nature photos. Try capturing your own nature scenes in glorious black and white.

haiku: Japanese poetry form that often incorporates nature themes. [HYE-koo]

READ ALL ABOUT IT

Nature inspires poets, philosophers, scientists, and artists. Even when you can't be outside in nature, you can enjoy reading about it. Check out books by these two classic nature writers:

Henry David Thoreau. What would it be like to live in the woods for two years? Henry David Thoreau did just that. Then he wrote about it in *Walden*, published in 1854.

Spending only $28.13, Thoreau built a small cabin beside Walden Pond, near Concord, Massachusetts. "I went to the woods because I wished to live deliberately," Thoreau wrote. What do you think "living deliberately" means?

Thoreau calls the clear lake "earth's eye." He compares the trees surrounding it to slender eyelashes. He describes the skater insects, squirrels, and other wildlife. He tells how changing seasons affect life at the pond. *Walden* also tells a lot about Thoreau's outlook on life.

Rachel Carson. Rachel Carson felt passionate about nature. Working at the United States Fish and Wildlife Service, Carson got out in the field often. She wrote her observations in notebooks.

Carson felt there was something "infinitely healing" in the flow of tides, birds' migration, the seasons, and other "repeated refrains of nature." Carson's skill with words helped readers not only see, but feel, nature's

beauty. Her book, *The Sea Around Us*, won the National Book Award in 1952.

Carson's most controversial book was *Silent Spring*, published in 1962. It predicted environmental disaster if pesticide use was not cut back. Powerful pesticides, like DDT, indeed killed bugs that ate crops. But the chemicals also hurt birds and other animals. The book's solid research helped convince lawmakers later to ban DDT.

PLANT A WILDLIFE GARDEN

Nature is all around us—even at home. Make part of a yard at home or school into a wildlife garden.

Keep your local habitat in mind when planning a wildlife garden. If you live in Arizona or New Mexico, for example, a desert garden makes much more sense than a temperate forest.

Decide first what wildlife you want to attract. Then plan your plants accordingly. If you want Monarch butterflies, for example, you'll have to plant milkweed, because that's what Monarchs' caterpillars eat. Other butterflies' caterpillars like tall grasses. These include the Prairie Skipper, the Wood Nymph, and the Fiery Skipper butterflies.

Native plants are best. A local nursery, botanical society, or college agricultural extension program can give you suggestions. Native plants encourage native animals to flock to your garden. That can partly "restore" an area's ecological balance—even in a built-up neighborhood.

Get your plants from a local nursery or swap plants with a friend. Don't just go dig

GET ACTIVE!

Write Haiku

Japanese haiku
Is a form of poetry.
Nature themes abound.

The form has three lines—
Five syllables, then seven,
Then just five again.

Count on your fingers.
Then it's easier to hear
Each word's syllables.

Paint a word picture.
Then add another image.
Where do they lead you?

Use visual clues,
Sounds, smells, and textures as well.
Bring the scene alive.

Write your own haiku.
Paint nature scenes with your words.
Share them with your friends.

up wild plants. The idea is to add to natural beauty—not to rip it up. Also, if you dug up an endangered species, you could be committing a crime!

With luck, you'll be able to include plants that flower from early spring through late fall. Some plants, like sunflowers, even do double duty. During summer, the bright flowers' nectar attracts bees and butterflies. During fall, the seed heads are a tasty treat for goldfinches and other birds.

Don't "weed" your garden. After all, you want it to grow naturally. But do take care of it. If there's a drought, make sure the plants get enough water.

Avoid using pesticides in your wildlife garden. Rely instead on nature's own system of checks and balances. Yes, aphids are pesky sapsuckers. But give ladybugs a chance, and they'll control the aphids without harmful chemicals.

A feeder helps attract birds to any garden. Mount it on a metal pole to keep squirrels from stealing the bird food. Once you start stocking a bird feeder, be sure to keep it up. Birds in the area will rely on you! In return, watch their antics as they enjoy the seed and suet you share with them.

Your wildlife garden can be a beautiful nature spot. Enjoy planning it and spending time there.

GET ACTIVE!

Pine Cone Bird Feeder

Store-bought bird feeders are great for stocking seed. For an extra winter treat, hang this pine cone feeder.

You need:
waxed paper
1 large pine cone
string—24 inches (61 cm) long
peanut butter or suet
butter knife

1. Line your work area with waxed paper to make cleanup easier.
2. Fold the string in half. Slip the middle part around the pine cone about 1/2" (1 cm) in from the narrow edge. Wrap each end around the cone a few times and knot. About 9 inches (23 cm) of string should hang loose at each end.
3. Put 1/4 cup of peanut butter or suet into a small bowl. Use the knife to pack the peanut butter or suet into the grooves of the pine cone.
4. Hang your pine cone feeder from a tree branch. Within a day or so birds should stop by for a treat.

GLOSSARY

WORDS TO KNOW

acid rain: precipitation that is more acidic, or has a lower pH than normal, due to certain pollutants.

adaptation: feature that helps a species survive in its environment. [ad-ap-TAY-shun]

alien: not native to a specific habitat; foreign. [ALE-ee-en]

altitude: height above sea level. [AL-tih-tood]

archaeon: single-celled organism found near deep sea vents. [ar-KAY-on]

atmosphere: layers of air surrounding Earth from its surface up to space. [AT-moss-fear]

ballast: water a ship carries so it floats at the right level. [BAL-ast]

bark: outer covering of a tree.

bioaccumulate: process by which poisons travel through the food chain from one species to another. [BYE-oh-ah-KYOOM-yoo-late]

biologist: scientist who studies living things. [bye-OL-oh-jist]

canopy: layer of the rain forest near the top of most trees. [CAN-oh-pee]

carnivore: meat-eating animal. [KAR-nih-vor]

chlorophyll: green material in plants and certain bacteria that enables them to make their own food. [KLOR-oh-fill]

condensation: process by which water changes from a gas into a liquid. [con-den-SAY-shun]

coniferous: cone-bearing. [koh-NIFF-er-us]

deciduous: describing a plant that seasonally loses its leaves. [dee-SID-yoo-us]

desert: a dry habitat that receives less than 10 inches (25 cm) of precipitation annually. [DEZ-ert]

digestion: process of breaking food down into useful nutrients. [dye-JES-chun]

DNA: deoxyribonucleic acid, which is the chemical in each cell that contains its genetic information.

earthquake: release of energy inside Earth, generally caused by tectonic plates scraping or sliding against each other.

echinoderm: spiny-skinned sea animal, such as a sea star. [ee-KINE-oh-derm]

echolocation: method bats use to locate prey with sound waves. [EK-oh-loh-CAY-shun]

ecological niche: an organism's "place" in its habitat, such as the time of day it's active or its specific feeding pattern. [EEK-oh-loj-ik-ul NISH]

eliminate: get rid of. [ee-LIM-in-ate]

emergent layer: vertical layer of the rain forest that only the tallest trees reach. [ee-MERJ-ent LAY-er]

ephemeral: short-lived. [ee-FEM-er-ul]

estivation: extended state of inactivity during periods of extreme heat. [ess-tih-VAY-shun]

evaporation: process by which liquid water changes into water vapor. [ee-vap-or-AY-shun]

fault lines: borders between tectonic plates.

floor: when used in connection with the rain forest, the lowest layer at which living things thrive.

food chain: term used to describe who-eats-whom relationships in nature.

food pyramid: method for depicting how certain organisms in a habitat support other organisms higher up on the pyramid.

food web: term used to describe multiple relationships among predators and prey in nature.

forb: catch-all phrase for plants that aren't trees or bushes; the term includes plants such as herbs and wildflowers.

fungus: member of a kingdom of living things that can be single or multi-celled, but which do not make their own food. [FUNG-us]

gametophyte: the life stage of a fern resulting from asexual reproduction; other organisms have gametophyte stages too. [ga-MET-oh-fite]

gill: structure on fish and certain other animals for extracting dissolved oxygen from water.

global warming: gradual increase in Earth's overall average annual temperatures, believed to result from increasing concentrations of carbon dioxide and other "greenhouse gases" in the atmosphere.

habitat: environment in which a living thing makes its home. [HAB-ih-tat]

haiku: Japanese poetry form that often incorporates nature themes. [HYE-koo]

herbivore: plant-eating animal. [ER-bih-vor]

hibernation: process by which warm-blooded animals slow their body processes to conserve energy and survive winter cold. [hye-ber-NAY-shun]

hydrofoil: aerodynamic shape that creates pressure differences in a fluid. [HYE-droh-foyl]

hydrometer: instrument used to measure a liquid's specific gravity [hye-DROM-et-er]

invertebrate: animal with no backbone. [in-VER-teh-brate]

keystone species: an organism upon which a significant number of other species depend for their survival in a particular habitat.

kilogram: metric measure of weight, equal to 1,000 grams. [KILL-oh-gram]

lichen: fungus and algae that grow together as if they were one organism. [LYE-ken]

liter: metric measure of volume, equal to approximately 1.056 liquid quarts. [LEE-ter]

marsupial: type of mammal that carries newborn young in a pouch. [mar-SOOP-ee-ul]

mass: how much matter something has.

metabolism: process by which a living thing gets some sort of food into its cells and turns it into energy. [meh-TAB-oh-lism]

metamorphosis: significant change in body form as an organism changes from an immature animal into an adult [met-uh-MOR-foh-siss]

meteor: flash of light that occurs when dust or rock from space, called meteoroids, burns up in Earth's atmosphere. [MEET-ee-or]

migration: seasonal travel pattern for animals. [mye-GRAY-shun]

mollusk: type of marine invertebrate, often having a shell. [MOL-usk]

monocot: category of plants that includes grasses. [MONN-oh-cot]

nocturnal: active at night. [nock-TER-nul]

oblate ellipsoid: geometrical term to describe Earth's squashed sphere shape. [OHB-late ee-LIP-soyd]

organism: a living thing. [OR-gun-ism]

parasite: an organism that feeds off another without giving its host any benefit. [PAIR-uh-site]

permafrost: permanently frozen ground. [PER-muh-frost]

pesticide: product designed to kill harmful insects or other organisms. [PESS-tih-side]

phloem: vascular tubes in a tree trunk that bring food to the rest of the plant. [FLOW-em]

photosynthesis: process by which an organism with chlorophyll makes food in the presence of sunlight and water. [FOH-toh-SIN-the-siss]

phytoplankton: tiny water-dwelling plants and bacteria that make their own food. [fye-toh-PLANK-tun]

pollinate: spread flower pollen in a way that helps the plant reproduce. [POL-in-ate]

prairie: type of grassland found on the Great Plains of North America. [PRAY-ree]

precipitation: collective term for rain, snow, sleet, hail, or other forms of water falling to Earth. [pree-SIP-ih-TAY-shun]

predator: animal that hunts another for food. [PRED-ah-tor]

prey: animal that is hunted by another for food. [PRAY]

propulsion: forward movement, as by pushing. [proh-PUL-shun]

Rayleigh scattering: process by which molecules in the atmosphere split or scatter different colors within white light. [RALL-ee SKAT-er-ing]

regenerate: regrow. [ree-JEN-er-ATE]

reproduce: process by which a living thing duplicates itself and/or its cells. [ree-proh-DOOS]

respiration: extracting oxygen from the air and getting it to cells; breathing. [res-pihr-AY-shun]

savanna: type of grassland where coarse grasses grow in patches, such as that found in tropical Africa. [suh-VAN-uh]

species: a specific type of living thing; the most specific level of description in taxonomy. The term generally describes organisms that reproduce only by themselves or with each other in nature to produce fertile offspring. [SPEE-shees]

specific gravity: measure of a material's density compared to distilled water.

sprawl: growth of urban and suburban areas into formerly rural areas.

steppe: dry grassland, such as that found in eastern Europe and western Asia.

sustainable development: economic growth that can continue to produce income year after year. [sus-TANE-uh-bul dee-VEL-up-ment]

symbiotic: mutually beneficial. [sim-bye-OT-ik]

taxonomy: scientific classification of living things. [TAX-on-oh-mee]

tectonic plates: large masses of Earth that "float" on top of the mantle. [tec-TONN-ik PLATES]

thorax: middle part of an animal's body (as on an insect); chest. [THOR-ax]

torpor: sluggish inactivity. [TORR-por]

tsunami: giant wave, usually caused by an earthquake or volcanic eruption. [SOO-nam-ee]

tundra: cold habitat found in northern polar regions or alpine areas. [TUN-druh]

ultraviolet: light wavelengths shorter than the visible spectrum. [ULL-tra-VYE-let]

understory: layer of the rain forest above the floor and beneath the canopy.

undulation: back-and-forth or sideways motion to propel oneself through water. [un-doo-LAY-shun]

vacuum: empty space. [VACK-yoo-um]

vascular: relating to tubes that transport liquid within an organism. [VAS-kyeh-lehr]

vertebrate: animal with a backbone. [VER-teh-brate]

volcano: land or underwater formation where pressure has pushed molten rock through the Earth's crust. [vol-KAY-noh]

wetlands: areas that are covered by water all or part of the year, or which are characterized by certain types of organisms.

xylem: vascular tubes in tree trunk that carry water from the roots through the rest of the plant. [ZYE-lem]

zooplankton: tiny water-dwelling, single-celled organisms and animals that do not make their own food. [zoh-oh-PLANK-tun]

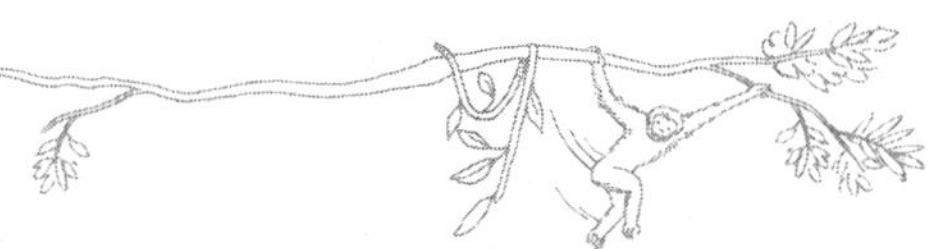

YOUNG ANIMALS

Adult	*Young Animal*
Bear	Cub
Beaver	Kitten
Caribou	Calf
Deer	Fawn
Duck	Duckling
Eagle	Eaglet
Eel	Elver
Elephant	Calf
Falcon	Eyas
Fish	Fry or Fingerling
Frog	Tadpole or Pollywog
Goat	Kid
Goose	Gosling
Insect	Nymph or Pupa
Kangaroo	Joey
Lion	Cub
Ostrich	Chick
Otter	Whelp
Rabbit	Bunny
Rhinoceros	Calf
Sea Lion	Pup
Shark	Cub
Sheep	Lamb
Swan	Cygnet
Tiger	Cub
Toad	Tadpole
Whale	Calf
Zebra	Foal

LOTS OF ANIMALS

What do you call a whole lot of animals? It depends. Here are some words for animal groups:

Colony of ants

Hive or swarm of bees

Army of caterpillars

Herd of elephants, caribou, or horses

Gang of elks

School of fish

Gaggle of geese

Horde of gnats

Nest of hornets

Mob or troop of kangaroos

Leap of leopards

Pride of lions

Swarm of locusts

Bed of oysters

Covey or bevy of quail

Knot of toads

Bale of turtles

Nest of vipers

Pack of wolves

RESOURCES

SELECTED INTERNET SITES

The Internet has hundreds of sites about nature topics. Here are a few sites to start your Internet safari. Make sure you have your parent's or guardian's permission to use the Internet. Also be sure you surf safely. Keep facts about your name, age, address, and phone number private.

Creature World
http://www.pbs.org/kratts/world/content.html
Click on the map and this PBS site gives you information about species around the world.

Desert Ecology
http://www.nps.gov/moja/mojade.htm
This site sponsored by the Mojave National Preserve has facts and photos about deserts in North America and around the world.

Endangered Animals
http://www.kidinfo.com/Science/Endangered_animals.html
Links to lots of sites with information about endangered animals.

Kids Corner, Endangered Species, U.S. Fish & Wildlife Service
http://www.fws.gov/r9endspp/kid_cor/kid_cor.htm
Interactive page with games, animal information, and more.

Mad Scientist Network
http://www.madsci.org
Includes fun experiments, vast archives, and Ask a Scientist feature.

National Wildlife Federation
http://www.nwf.org
Read about endangered species and habitats, and find out how the National Wildlife Federation wants to protect them.

ParkNet: Gateway to the National Park Service
http://www.nps.gov
Find out about the wide world of beauty and historical heritage in America's national parks.

Rainforest Action Network
http://www.ran.org/kids_action/index1.html
Question and answer section, species information, and ways to help the rain forest.

Sea World/Busch Gardens Animal Resources
http://www.seaworld.org/infobook.html
Facts and information about the oceans and animals worldwide.

U.S. EPA Explorers' Club
http://www.epa.gov/kids
Fun stuff for kids who want to explore and care for the environment.

U.S. EPA Student Center
http://www.epa.gov/students
Neat resources on conservation, ecosystems, water, air, recycling, and other topics.

Zoological Society of San Diego
http://www.sandiegozoo.org
Includes a learning outpost with photos and information about lots of plants and animals.

ORGANIZATIONS

American Forests
P.O. Box 2000
Washington, DC 20013
202/955-4500
http://www.amfor.org or *http://www.american-forests.org*

Greenpeace International and Greenpeace USA
1436 U Street, NW
Washington, DC 20009
800/326-0959
http://www.greenpeace.org

National Arbor Day Foundation
100 Arbor Avenue
Nebraska City, NE 68410
402/474-5655
http://www.arborday.org

National Wildlife Federation
8925 Leesburg Pike
Vienna, VA 22184
703/790-4000
http://www.nwf.org

Nature Conservancy
4245 N. Fairfax Drive, Suite 100
Arlington, VA 22203-1606
800/628-6860
http://www.tnc.org

Sierra Club
85 Second Street, 2nd Floor
San Francisco, CA 94105
415/977-5500
http://www.sierraclub.org

United States Environmental Protection Agency
401 M Street, SW
Washington, DC 20460
202/260-4048
http://www.epa.gov

World Wildlife Fund
1250 24th Street, NW
Washington, DC 20077
800/225-5993
http://www.worldwildlife.org

SELECTED READING

There are hundreds of books and articles to help you learn more about nature. Here are a few suggestions:

Ackerman, Diane. *Bats: Shadows in the Night*. New York: Crown Publishers, 1997.

Allaby, Michael. *Deserts*. Biomes of the World Series. Danbury, CT: Grolier Educational, 1999.

Bennett, Paul. *Communicating*. New York: Thomson Learning, 1995.

Bramwell, Martyn. *Nature*. New York: Warwick Press, 1989.

Bredeson, Carmen. *Tide Pools*. New York: Franklin Watts, 1999.

Burnie, David. *101 Nature Experiments: A Step-by-Step Guide*. London: Dorling Kindersley, 1996.

Carnegie Library of Pittsburgh. *The Handy Science Answer Book*. Detroit: Visible Ink, 1997.

Children's School of Science. *The Big Book of Nature Projects: 53 Terrific Experiments, Field Trips, and Activities for Kids*. New York: Thames & Hudson, Inc., 1997.

Clark, John. *Seas and Oceans*. New York: Aladdin Books, 1992.

Cooper, Ann. *Above the Treeline*. Denver, CO: Denver Museum of Natural History Press, 1996.

d'Elgin, Tershia. *The Everything Bird Book*. Holbrook, MA: Adams Media Corp., 1998.

Else, George, et al., eds. *Insects & Spiders*. New York: Time-Life Books, 1997.

George, Michael. *Tundra*. Mankato, MN: Creative Education, 1994.

Goldstein, Natalie. *Rebuilding Prairies and Forests*. Chicago: Childrens Press, 1994.

Goodman, Billy. *The Rain Forest*. Boston: Little Brown, 1996.

Gutnik, Marin J., and Natalie Browne-Gutnik. *Great Barrier Reef*. Austin, TX: Raintree Steck-Vaughn, 1995.

Hewitt, Sally. *All Kinds of Habitats*. New York: Children's Press, 1999.

Inseth, Zachary. *The Tundra*. Chanhassen, MN: Child's World, Inc., 1999.

Johnson, Darv. *The Amazon Rain Forest*. San Diego: Lucent Books, 1999.

Lambert, David. *The Kingfisher Young People's Book of Oceans*. New York: Larousse Kingfisher Chambers, 1997.

Lesinski, Jeanne M. *Exotic Invaders*. New York: Walker, 1996.

Llamas, Andreu. *The Vegetation of Rivers, Lakes, and Swamps*. New York: Chelsea House Pubs., 1996.

Macquitty, Miranda. *Desert*. London: Dorling Kindersley, 1994.

Martin, James. *Hiding Out: Camouflage in the Wild*. New York: Crown Publishers, 1993.

Miller, Arthur P., and Marjorie L. Miller. *Park Ranger Guide to Seashores*. Harrisburg, PA: Stackpole Books, 1992.

National Wildlife Federation. *Discovering Deserts*. Philadelphia: Chelsea House, 1999.

Parker, Steve, ed. *Natural World*. London: Dorling Kindersley, 1994.

Perham, Molly, and Julian Rowe. *Mapworlds: Wildlife*. Danbury, CT: Franklin Watts, 1997.

Peterson Field Guide Series. Boston: Houghton Mifflin. [Various dates and subjects].

Pipes, Rose. *Tundra and Cold Deserts*. Austin, TX: Raintree Steck-Vaughn, 1999.

Ricciuti, Edward R. *Desert*. New York: Benchmark Books, 1996.

Ruth, Maria Mudd. *The Deserts of the Southwest*. New York: Benchmark Books, 1999.

Sayre, April Pulley. *Desert*. New York: Twenty-First Century Books, 1994.

Sayre, April Pulley. *Tropical Rain Forest*. New York: Twenty-First Century Books, 1994.

Sayre, April Pulley. *Ocean*. New York: Twenty-First Century Books, 1996.

Scott, Michael. *The Young Oxford Book of Ecology*. New York: Oxford University Press, 1995.

Seddon, Tony, and Jill Bailey. *The Living World*. Garden City, NY: Doubleday & Co., 1987.

Starr, Cecie, and Ralph Taggart. *Biology: The Unity and Diversity of Life*. 8th ed. Belmont, CA: Wadsworth Pub. Co., 1998.

Staub, Frank. *America's Prairies*. Minneapolis: Carolrhoda Books, 1994.

Staub, Frank. *America's Wetlands*. Minneapolis: Carolrhoda Books, 1995.

Taylor, Barbara. *Desert Life*. New York: Covent Gardens Books, 1998.

Telford, Carole, and Rod Theodorous. *Inside a Coral Reef*. Des Plaines, IL: Heinemann Interactive Library, 1998.

Tucker, Priscilla M. *Basic Nature Projects: 101 Fun Explorations*. Mechanicsburg, PA: Stackpole Books, 1995.

VanCleave, Janice. *Oceans for Every Kid: Easy Activities That Make Learning Science Fun*. New York: John Wiley & Sons, Inc., 1996.

INDEX

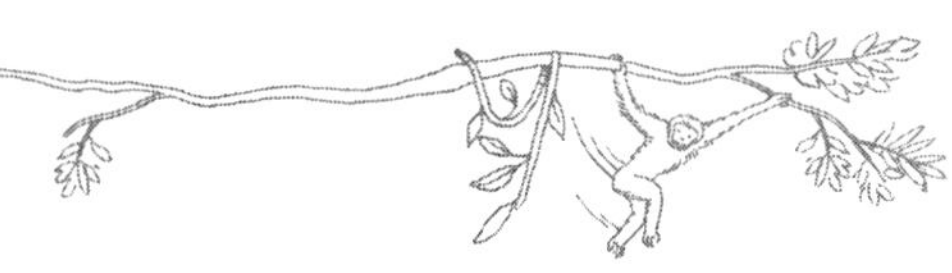

M

O

P

R

S

T

U

V

W

X

Y

Z

We Have EVERYTHING!

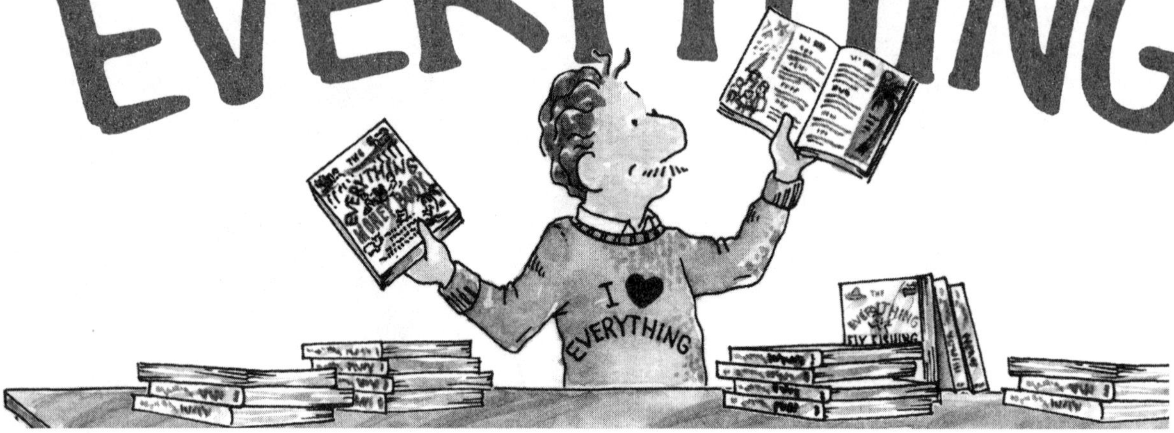

Available wherever books are sold!

Everything **After College Book**
$12.95, 1-55850-847-3

Everything **Astrology Book**
$12.95, 1-58062-062-0

Everything **Baby Names Book**
$12.95, 1-55850-655-1

Everything **Baby Shower Book**
$12.95, 1-58062-305-0

Everything **Barbeque Cookbook**
$12.95, 1-58062-316-6

Everything® **Bartender's Book**
$9.95, 1-55850-536-9

Everything **Bedtime Story Book**
$12.95, 1-58062-147-3

Everything **Beer Book**
$12.95, 1-55850-843-0

Everything **Bicycle Book**
$12.95, 1-55850-706-X

Everything **Build Your Own Home Page**
$12.95, 1-58062-339-5

Everything **Casino Gambling Book**
$12.95, 1-55850-762-0

Everything **Cat Book**
$12.95, 1-55850-710-8

Everything® **Christmas Book**
$15.00, 1-55850-697-7

Everything **College Survival Book**
$12.95, 1-55850-720-5

Everything **Cover Letter Book**
$12.95, 1-58062-312-3

Everything **Crossword and Puzzle Boo**
$12.95, 1-55850-764-7

Everything **Dating Book**
$12.95, 1-58062-185-6

Everything **Dessert Book**
$12.95, 1-55850-717-5

Everything **Dog Book**
$12.95, 1-58062-144-9

Everything **Dreams Book**
$12.95, 1-55850-806-6

Everything **Etiquette Book**
$12.95, 1-55850-807-4

Everything **Family Tree Book**
$12.95, 1-55850-763-9

Everything **Fly-Fishing Book**
$12.95, 1-58062-148-1

Everything **Games Book**
$12.95, 1-55850-643-8

Everything **Get-a-Job Book**
$12.95, 1-58062-223-2

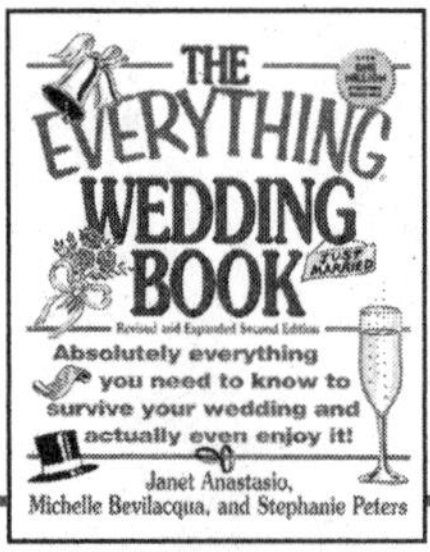

$12.95, 384 pages, 8" x 9 1/4"

The ultimate reference for couples planning their wedding!

- Scheduling, budgeting, etiquette, hiring caterers, florists, and photographers
- Ceremony & reception ideas
- Over 100 forms and checklists
- And much, much more!

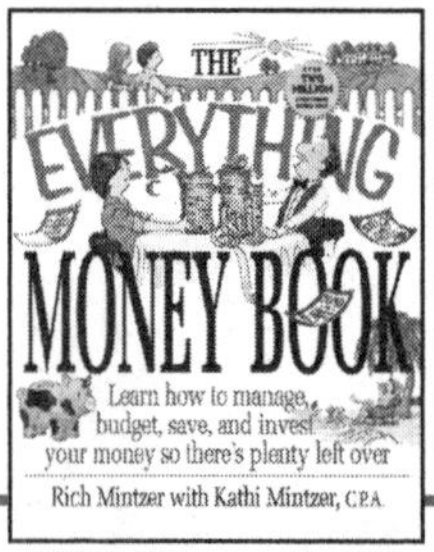

$12.95, 288 pages, 8" x 9 1/4"

Personal finance made easy—and fun!

- Create a budget you can live with
- Manage your credit cards
- Set up investment plans
- Money-saving tax strategies
- And much, much more!

For more information, or to order, call 800-872-5627
or visit www.adamsmedia.com/everything

Adams Media Corporation, 260 Center Street, Holbrook, MA 02343

EVERYTHING

Trade paperback, $9.95
1-58062-322-0, 144 pages

The Everything Kids' Money Book

by Diane Mayr

From allowances to money gifts, from lemonade stands to lawn-mowing businesses, *The Everything Kids' Money Book* tells kids how to make money, save money, and spend money. It also has fascinating information about currency, an introduction to the stock market, and even some fun money-based games. Basically, this book is filled with everything a kid would want to know about money.

The Everything Kids' Puzzle Book

by Jennifer A. Ericsson & Beth L. Blair

Stuck inside on a rainy day? Trapped in a car for a long trip? Just love puzzles? This is your book! From crosswords to mazes to picture puzzles, this book is filled with hours of puzzling fun. As an added bonus, every space that doesn't have a puzzle in it is filled with fascinating facts and funny jokes. You'll never be bored with *The Everything Kids' Puzzle Book* by your side!

Trade paperback, $9.95
1-58062-323-9, 160 pages

Available wherever books are sold.

For more information, or to order, call 800-872-5627
or visit www.adamsmedia.com

Adams Media Corporation, 260 Center Street, Holbrook, MA 02343